"HAUNTED LOUISVILLE" AND LOUISVILLE GHOST WALKS

Whether you are a Louisville resident who likes to read about local hauntings or a person who enjoys a good ghost story about any location, you will definitely want a copy of Robert Parker's Haunted Louisville for your collection. Known as Louisville's Mr. Ghost Walker, Robert recounts true stories about many downtown sites both on the walking tour and in this book. The "spirited stories" from the tour are not lost in the written version! This book reflects the research and retelling of unique stories you won't find anywhere else. It is a rare combination of information and entertainment that is universal in its appeal. Haunted Louisville should be at the top of every ghost lover's "must have" list.

ROBERTA SIMPSON BROWN — AUTHOR, STORYTELLER & GHOST HUNTER

Haunted Louisville features Robert's feet-on-the-ground familiarity with years of ghost tours at over a dozen downtown spooky sites. Robert Parker reports on the scary panorama of Louisville-intriguing the believers and mystifying the skeptical. Haunted Louisville is a trifecta of enjoyment in terms of history, hauntings and the personality of Mr. Ghost Walker himself.

**THOMAS FREESE — AUTHOR OF SHAKER GHOST STORIES &
FOG SWIRLER AND 11 OTHER GHOST STORIES**

On warm summer evenings you can find Mr. Ghost Walker probing the depths of the spirit realm in downtown Louisville, Kentucky. Detailed accounts and eyewitness testimony gives credibility to the idea that the dead walk among us. You too can enjoy the spellbinding sensation as your own skepticism gives way when the spirits make contact with you. Will you believe?

JUSTIN WILSON — LINDSAY WILSON COLLEGE ALUMNI CORRESPONDENT

it's Parker's storytelling that is the treat of the tour- the meat and bones that make it worthwhile. These days, oral histories tend to be embodied in some sort of electronic device, so it's a wonderful throwback to hear ghost stories straight from the mouth of Parker.

LEO WEEKLY MAGAZINE

As the years passed and the buildings have gotten older, stories are being told that maybe some of our Louisville ancestors have not left. They remain with us, giving us glimpses into their lives.

SHARON BROWN — LOUISVILLE GHOST HUNTERS SOCIETY

Ghosts & Hauntings from Downtown Louisville's Most Famous Addresses

HAUNTED LOUISVILLE
History & Hauntings of the Derby City
ROBERT W. PARKER

Robert Parker

- A Whitechapel Press Book from Dark Haven Entertainment -

I'd like to dedicate my first book, 'Haunted Louisville', to several people who have been instrumental in this project:

Lonnie and Roberta Brown, good friends, who were always ready to go on my wild-goose chases to visit properties that were reported to be haunted; with guided words they counseled, and listened to all my stories and ideas with their undying support.

Corn Island Storytelling of Kentucky Festival, and the volunteers who freely gave their time to support Mr. Ghost Walker and the ghost tours. Thanks!

My family and friends have been present with words of encouragement to keep the spirit alive.

My friend Bill, of St. Louis, MO, who looked at every single one of my photographs and who assisted with the transfer of the photography onto CDs.

Three cheers for everyone who had anything to do with this project of collecting the downtown Louisville ghost stories -- for that, I'm grateful.

Original Cover Artwork Designed by
© Copyright 2007 by Michael Schwab & Troy Taylor
Visit M & S Graphics at http://www.manyhorses.com

Original Photographs by Robert W. Parker
Additional Photograph Credits: William Storer

This Book is Published By:
Whitechapel Press
A Division of Dark Haven Entertainment, Inc.
15 Forest Knolls Estates - Decatur, Illinois - 62521
(217) 422-1002 / 1-888-GHOSTLY
Visit us on the internet at http://www.prairieghosts.com

First Edition -- May 2007
ISBN: 1-892523-51-5

WELCOME TO HAUNTED LOUISVILLE!

The history of Louisville spans hundreds of years and, thanks to its shadowy past and its unusual location, is home to hundreds of ghosts and legends. The first settlement here dates back to 1778 and was founded by Colonel George Rogers Clark, a hero of the Revolutionary War. In 1803, two other American heroes passed through Louisville - Meriwether Lewis and William Clark, who used the settlement to organize their expedition to the American West.

The city's dark history includes its traffic in slaves before the Civil War. It had one of the largest slave trades in America and much of its early growth was based on the revenue gained from it. Ironically, Louisville was also a major stop on the Underground Railroad, which offered passage to slaves escaping to freedom in the north as soon as they crossed the Ohio River.

During the Civil War, Louisville was a stronghold for Federal forces, which kept Kentucky in the Union. It became a center for planning, supplies, recruiting and transportation during numerous campaigns. By the end of the war, Louisville had never been attacked, even though several battles occurred nearby. On March 27, 1890, the city was devastated, and the downtown nearly destroyed, by a horrific tornado. Nearly 100 people were killed and while the city was quickly rebuilt, the event left a lasting impact on Louisville.

During the early 1900s, Louisville had one of the highest tuberculosis death rates in the country. Thanks to the swampy river ground, the "White Death" ran rampant, leading to the construction of the Waverly Hills Sanatorium. The hospital was opened in 1926 and operated until 1961. Thousands died during this years, leading the hospital to become known as one of the most haunted places in the country.

In the late winter of 1937, a month of heavy rain deluged the city and is still remembered as the "Great Flood of 37". The flood submerged a huge part of the city, knocking out power and forcing the evacuation of more than 175,000 residents. The city saw many changes in the coming years, including new flood walls and strong growth in the high elevations of the region.

Today, Louisville is seen as one of the grand cities of the mid-south, home to the Kentucky Derby and much more. It is also recognized as one of America's most haunted cities - a fact that will become increasingly apparent in the pages ahead!

TABLE OF CONTENTS

INTRODUCTION

Four years ago, the character of Mr. Ghost Walker was created to lead folks on historical walking tours of downtown Louisville and each story told had a ghostly slant. The plan was to use the walks as a fundraiser for the Corn Island Storytelling Festival of Kentucky.

The inaugural tour brought the usual nervousness and anxiety. Not knowing exactly what to expect on this first night, it was difficult to prepare. The doors at the Kentucky Theater opened up for business and we waited, and waited, and waited. Much to our dismay, only three walkers were present. I felt guilty charging the three people money. The stories were short but the content was still the same. Ghosts do haunt the older buildings in downtown Louisville.

The event turned out well. Their comments were favorable and full of encouragement. The next walk that was scheduled went very well, and had much better attendance.

When the ghost walks started, I served as a local historian and as a guy who had learned the ghost story legends associated with the building. Now, three years later, I've witnessed several events that have made a believer out of me when it comes to hauntings.

My mission in this writing is to share some of the events with you and to reinforce that there is a world on the 'other side'.

One such event occurred early in my career as Mr. Ghost Walker. I was invited to accompany a group of serious ghost investigators to the Waverly Hills Sanatorium in southwest Jefferson County. Waverly was a tuberculosis hospital where over 63,000 people died. Many consider it to be one of the most haunted places in the world. Some members in the crowd included the Discovery Channel and MTV, as well as some authors and researchers of the paranormal.

It had rained the night prior to our visit and puddles had accumulated on the cafeteria floor. Since it wasn't totally dark outdoors, our guide had allowed us a few minutes to simply explore on our own in that area. Two or three of us had gathered around the perimeter of a large puddle on the floor and were discussing the events of the evening. Unknown to us, some form of a being passed between us as we were standing there. The only feeling was a slight wisp of cold air, yet the surface of the water was undisturbed. But what caught my attention left an impression that I'll never forget.

On the floor near where we were standing, bare footprints began appearing, one after another, as if the ghost was walking away from us. The first footprint showed the shape of the bare foot, complete with five toes, the contour of the foot, and the heel. As the first step manifested itself, we stood in amazement and disbelief. What soon followed were four more footprints. Each one grew fainter than the previous. The last footprint only revealed the big toe and the heel. We made side-by-side comparisons of the first footprint and our own feet. We made the assumption that the footprint belonged to that of a female, for it was too small to be male.

That was the first encounter that I have ever witnessed where the paranormal made itself known in a simple way. And it wasn't the last, either.

A year passed from that first encounter, and some friends and I were visiting another haunted property in southern Indiana. We were taking a candlelight tour of the Culbertson Mansion in New Albany, Indiana. Since the Culbertson Mansion is a historical home and state park, the state will only allow ghost stories to be told during the month of October.

On that particular night, I was on a tour with about 20 other guests. Most of them were already spooked prior to reaching the second floor master bedroom of the mansion. Our guide, a delightful woman who was knowledgeable about the ghostly activities, had led us into the master bedroom on the second floor. She began explaining to us that the furniture we were seeing wasn't actual furniture used by the Culbertson family, but period antiques used to make the home look more natural.

The guide focused our attention on the bed and the white linen bed covering.

"Both the bed and the bedspread are well over 100 years old," she said, "and the bedspread is never touched without the docent wearing white cotton gloves."

She stressed to us that the Culbertsons never slept on this bed, nor did they ever use the bedspread as a covering.

She began to explain ghostly activity in the room, two of which involved the bed. One form of evidence was the shape left behind of someone who had been sitting on the bedside, and his or her form was seen in the bedspread. Just that statement scared several of the guests and they vacated the room and huddled together in the hallway. That left about five of us in the room. Our guide continued her narration, and said that the second form of evidence is a handprint that will appear in the bed.

In silence, we all stared at the bedspread, and the covering was completely smooth. As our guide directed our attention elsewhere in the room, a guest interrupted her presentation.

She exclaimed, "I see a handprint in the bed!"

Yes, a handprint had appeared on the left side of the bed -- a handprint that wasn't there before. That frightened the remaining five women and they scurried to the hallway and joined the others.

Looking at the guide, I said, "May I come closer to the bed and take some photographs?"

She gave me permission to do so and dropped the red velvet rope. I moved close to the left side of the bed and knelt down. Once I reached the floor and was on one knee, I hurriedly began taking photographs. My excitement was building from seeing this handprint. As I was photographing the handprint from various angles, I felt two hands on my shoulders but I never turned around to see the big hands that felt so cold. I just reasoned that someone in the party had returned and was looking over my shoulder. But whoever it was had strong, muscular hands, for I could clearly sense the fingers on the front of my shoulders and the thumbs on my back.

After taking several pictures, I rose and felt the strangest sensation sweep through my body. I can only compare it to a tingling that one would feel after a period of numbness on the body. It raced from my feet, up through my legs, past my hips, through my abdomen, and it seemed to just shoot out my shoulders. I recall looking around the room and saw only the guide placing the red velvet rope back onto its holder. My steps were staggered, as if I were intoxicated. My knees were weak and felt as if they were going to collapse under my own weight.

I made my way into the next room and joined the others who were listening to the presentation. Holding onto the door facing, I spotted a chair and made my way to it. My head tilted back and hit the wall. My eyes were focused on the ceiling. I could hear the presentation clearly, but wasn't able to look about the room. After several deep breaths, I was able to relax and place my head back into the normal body position. My guide had finished her presentation and I motioned for her to come over to me.

"When we were next to the bed, who came over and put their hands on my shoulders?" I asked her.

"Nobody touched you," she replied.

"Oh, yes they did! I felt two large hands on my shoulders; big hands, cold fingers, and I could even feel the thumbs on my back. Somebody touched me!" I explained.

She interrupted my speech and said, "Oh, lordy, it had to have been the ghost of Mr. Culbertson! That room has had a lot of activity and he was such a tall and strong man! I bet he touched you!"

"Whoever it was just pulled the energy from my body, for I feel like I'm exhausted," I told her. "It didn't feel like it was going to push me over, or pull me back, or even rock me left or right. I never felt fear when I stood up. But something or someone had their hands on my body."

Could it have been Mr. Culbertson? I don't know and probably won't ever know. I do know that ghost investigators have talked about ghosts that want to make contact with you and when they do, they will pull the energy out of your body. The presence that touched me pulled the energy out of my body. That must be the case here for it was a sensation that I'd never felt before.

In this book, you'll be reading accounts of what employees have witnessed and stories that have been passed on by word of mouth. Does Mr. Brown haunt his own hotel? Are the Brennans lingering in their Italian-style mansion after all of these years?

You can draw your own conclusions from reading each story about the mysteries of each property. And when you do reach a conclusion, be sure to share them with Mr. Ghost Walker. He can be found wherever ghosts can be found!

Robert W. Parker
Haunted Louisville Kentucky
May 2007

1. PAMELA BROWN'S TRAGEDY

Actor's Theater
320 Main Street

Driving west on Main Street, a motorist would hardly notice the gray stone structure with the two gigantic Ionic columns out front. Since 1837, it has housed several banks and a credit union. During 1930 to 1937, the building sat empty until the Louisville Credit Men's Association moved in.

In 1972, Actor's Theater purchased the old Bank of Louisville property. John Y. Brown, Jr., donated a generous gift in the memory of his sister, Pamela Brown, to financially underwrite the theater's construction and remodeling. They built a theater behind the present building. Patrons of the theater today stand in the lobby of the once former bank and admire the decorated ceiling and skylight.

Three doors are on the southern end of the lobby. The door on the right opens to the original vault for the bank. Theatergoers can exit through two of the remaining doors to reach the auditorium. The door on the left leads to the balcony. The remaining center door leads to the main floor of the auditorium, named for Pamela Brown, that seats 637 guests. There is a passageway that is lined with brown bricks and is dimly lit and this contains a bust of Pamela Brown. And it is also believed that she haunts the theater.

Recently, I joined a group of educators on a tour of the theater. I was hoping for a glimpse of Pamela Brown's spirit. If she did not appear in ghostly form, I felt that part of her would always make itself felt there because of the love that she had for the place.

"I've been leading tours of the theater for a number of years," the guide began, while walking across the stage. "Countless numbers of actors have performed on this stage, and each with fond memories of being received by the audience with rounds of applause. However, we have one character that makes a few visible appearances, but the eye has to be watching."

She lowered her right index finger that was pointed to her eye and continued. She moved closer to the edge of the stage as we educators watched and listened to her soft-spoken words. She raised both hands toward the ceiling and looked up into the openness of spotlights and narrow catwalks.

In a dramatic monologue, she continued, "For just as the house lights go down, another spectral performance just might begin."

At that, she began lowering her hands until they folded against her long yellow skirt. We waited with breathless anticipation until she began her story.

"An African-American male has been spotted backstage. At first, it was assumed that he was an employee, or a backstage delivery person, or contract laborer. Since then, we've changed our minds about that. Little is known of this man. We have no name or identity. His appearance is of a grayish silhouette that seems to wonder the backstage area and in the lower level of the building. He's been seen with enough frequency that we have been able to identity his features of African descent. He's a tall man and wanders about with heavy footsteps that pound against the floor. Whether he was involved in the theater remains a mystery. Perhaps he was involved with the building during its early years, going back to the late 1800s, and is displaced, lost in time. Nobody knows. He's made no contact with anyone and it seems like once he realizes that he's been discovered, he simply vanishes from sight."

But another apparition has also been seen. It is a woman who has a connection to this theater. The spirit, who has an uncanny resemblance to the likeness of the bust in the foyer and the portrait in the lobby, is believed to be Pamela Brown Anderson. But nobody is sure. Pamela's story is sad and has a tragic end.

Out of respect for the Brown family, Pamela Brown Anderson's story will be told here as it has been presented to me. The readers of this passage can form their own conclusion as to whether the ghost that has been alluded to is the ghost of Pamela Brown Anderson, or if it is some other displaced and unknown spirit.

Anticipation filled the morning of September 20, 1970, in East Hampton, New York. The buzz surrounded a stunning 28-year-old actress from Louisville, Kentucky, by the name of Pamela Brown Anderson. Next to her was her 32-year-old husband, Rod Anderson, from New York. Rounding out the trio was an Englishman, Malcolm Brighton, who was their close friend and pilot.

With excitement in their voices and eyes wide open, the three were embarking on a history-making event of being the first to cross the Atlantic Ocean by balloon. Their dream was to write a book detailing the events of the journey and recoup the expenses of this undertaking by doing so. The three were patterning themselves after such historic explorers as Charles Lindbergh and Amelia Earhart. They were going to be famous and live forever in the history books as great American explorers.

The *Free Life* was their sailing vessel. The balloon rose to a height comparable to a seven-story building. It was designed in vivid colors of yellow, white, and orange.

The vessel became airborne amid the cheers and applause of the townspeople and news reporters. The spectators were all focused on the gigantic balloon that was ascending over the shores of Long Island.

Nobody gave thought to the unthinkable. Are the three experienced enough for such a project? Only time would tell.

It wasn't too long before problems occurred. The sheer joy shared by the crew turned to panic and fear.

On day two, an experimental hot-air mechanism, which was designed to maintain the correct altitude during nighttime hours failed. Another hardship was a dangerous rainstorm that was brought on by an unforeseen cold front.

Unfortunately, The *Free Life* was traveling on borrowed time. During the darkness of night, it went down into the cold and tormented waters of the Atlantic Ocean. The passengers were never to be seen or heard from again. Radar estimated that The *Free Life* went down about 600 miles southeast of Newfoundland.

On Tuesday morning, every newspaper in the country broke headlines with the fatal story of the three who were lost at sea. Columnist Robert McFadden wrote in the *New York Times* under this title, "Balloon with 3 Atlantic Hop Feared Down at Sea."

Two men and a woman attempting the first transAtlantic crossing in a balloon were caught in a heavy rainstorm 500 miles east southeast of St. John's, Newfoundland, last night and radioed for assistance, saying they were preparing to ditch into the sea.

The last message from the balloon, received at 7:05 P.M. by Aeronautical Radio, Inc., a commercial radio service, said: 'Six hundred feet and descending. Signing off. Will try contact after landing.'

Immediately, a search party was activated by the Brown family. A command central was established in the Plaza Hotel on New York City's Fifth Avenue. Representatives from the Royal Canadian Air Force, the American Navy, and the Coast Guard searched for days without any success. Pamela's brother, John Y. Brown, financed a private search with a DC6 but after three weeks, he gave up the search.

Only a few remains of The *Free Life* were found. Some fragments from the gondola were plucked from the water's icy surface. Sadly, no evidence of Pamela,

Rod, and Malcolm were ever discovered. Their remains are still missing to this day.

One year later, in 1971, Actor's Theater had purchased the property on Main Street and was undertaking a $1.7 million dollar expansion. Their plan was to convert an older building into performance venues to house administrative offices and support for the theater.

John Y. Brown came forth with a generous gift to support Actor's Theater expansion.

"We hope that this gift will, in some small way, allow Pamela's memory to live on for all those who knew her. She lived and played her life in the theater," Brown stated.

Pamela had many talents, one of which was playing the harp. Her theatrical career was birthed in Louisville. She was involved with Shakespeare in the Park, where she had several roles in the productions of The Tempest, Twelfth Night, Macbeth, and Julius Caesar. Pamela was no stranger to theater here or elsewhere, and it truly was her lifeblood. She had a few appearances on national television, "The Ed Sullivan Show" and "The Lawrence Welk Show". From there, she transitioned to a standing character role on a popular soap opera of that time, "Love Is A Many Splendored Thing."

Genie Chipps, who was present at the launching of The Free Life and was a close friend, stated: "Theatrical legends were the things she most admired. Big, sweeping, dramatic productions were the things that inspired her."

If the ghost of Pamela Brown is haunting the theater that is so aptly named in her honor, it could only be a good thing to have her presence there.

2. SCREAMS IN THE STREAM

The Belle of Louisville
Fourth Street Wharf

The steamboat that Louisvillians know as the *Belle of Louisville* wasn't always the delightful excursion boat that we associate with today. Before she became the "Belle", this historic steamboat had other uses and other names.

When construction on the boat was completed in 1914, owner James Rees and Sons in Pittsburgh named her the *Idlewild*. Under this name, she was ready to begin the journey that would take her to many cities along the Ohio River Valley.

Built as a cargo ship, the *Idlewild* hauled cotton, lumber, and grain. However, during summer months in the 1920s, she doubled as an excursion boat, offering trips for passengers between Memphis, Tennessee, and West Memphis, Arkansas. She became known as a 'tramping' steamboat because the term 'tramp' was used when steamboats traveled from town to town doing summer excursions for tourists wanting to escape the heat. The *Idlewild* had many ports of call along the Ohio, Illinois, Mississippi, and Missouri rivers.

In 1931, the *Idlewild* docked in Louisville and was chartered by a resort called Rose Island. The *Idlewild* provided ferry service for passengers traveling to Fontaine Ferry Amusement Park in western Louisville to Rose Island in Indiana.

After a glorious career of carrying passengers, the *Idlewild* was placed in service during World War II. Her role was to push oil barges along the Ohio River. When time allowed, she became a floating USO facility for soldiers stationed at military installations along the river. As our country exited the World War II time period, life started to change for Louisvillians and, with it, so did the *Idlewild*.

During 1947, J. Herod Gorsage purchased the *Idlewild*. Mr. Gorsage had an association with a riverboat captain by the name of Ben Winters. Captain

Winters, who was 87-years-old, had been piloting a different steamboat by the name of Avalon. Now, Captain Winters began piloting the *Idlewild*.

On August 10, 1947, the *Idlewild* had reached Lacrosse, Wisconsin, for its final destination on that journey. Little did Captain Winters know that he would meet his final destination there, as well.

Rumors had been circulating that the *Idlewild* had been transporting illegal liquors and was supporting gambling and other devices of the day. When the Lacrosse sheriff raided the *Idlewild*, there was a struggle and Captain Winters said he refused to be taken alive from the steamboat. He got his wish. Captain Winters suffered a heart attack and died in the Captain's Quarters on the upper deck. It was his deathbed wish that the *Idlewild* be renamed the *Avalon*. Gorsage complied and the change was made in 1948.

Today, there are those who wonder if Captain Winters ever left the steamboat. They wonder if he haunts the *Belle of Louisville* thinking that it is still his beloved *Avalon*.

On a damp, chilly night in September of 2003, I was part of a group who took a special late night tour of the *Belle of Louisville*. Even though it is not officially haunted, we had all heard stories about many people who boarded this old-time paddle wheeler and encountered strange things that they could not explain. We didn't know that we were about to become part of that group. We just knew that the wind was biting at our faces and the murky Ohio River was lapping against the old steamboat like some mysterious living thing gnawing away at its sides. We were happy when we were escorted into the Captain's Quarters to hear some history about the boat. We gathered close, enjoying the warmth and brightness of the cheerful room. But the atmosphere suddenly change. As the guide was explaining to us about how Captain Winters met his death in the room, one of the lighted wall sconces went out. The room grew silent. Those of us standing there looked at one another in disbelief.

Our guide elaborated, "When we have sensed Captain Winters presence in this room, one or two of the lighted wall sconces go off."

Within twenty or thirty seconds, the light went back on. That was the first form of ghostly activity that we experienced in that room. It definitely wasn't the last, either.

After the short history lecture, we were free to roam about the boat and take pictures. I took several shots with my digital camera from various angles and then moved about the decks with a friend of mine, just letting the atmosphere sink into our imaginations. When doors were left open, we looked inside or stepped into the small rooms to see what we could find. Mostly, we were just trying to feel what it would be like to be a worker on the old boat.

In one suite of rooms, the atmosphere took on a distinct sinister feeling. The whitewashed walls of wainscot paneling soon transformed to a dismal gray shade as we stepped to the inner room. The temperature was noticeably colder than the temperature outside on deck. My friend and I both felt discomfort in the two rooms.

"I don't like it in here," was my first reaction.

As we moved back into the outer room, something sparkly caught my eye. I discovered, on the ledge of the wainscot paneling almost hidden away, a woman's ring! The diamond had a glitter that seemed to fade when I picked it up. Jokingly, I placed it upon my fifth finger. Immediately, I knew something eerie had possession of this ring. Coldness swept all over my right hand, much like a glove would warm someone's hand, yet my left hand felt normal.

"We're not welcome in this room," I exclaimed. "This ring needs to come off!" I promptly removed it and placed it back on the ledge where I found it.

"We need to leave immediately and say nothing of finding this ring to the others," I told my friend.

She agreed and we left at once. Outside, the two of us talked about what had just happened and agreed not to discuss it with the others.

Our presence disturbed something that was lurking in that room. It was unhappy with our intrusion. Some spirit had a connection to the diamond ring and, unknowingly, I had made contact with it. We later learned that this area was used as the "sick bay". Apparently, many former workers had suffered and even died in those two rooms. The connection to the ring remains a mystery to this day.

We continued on to the upper deck when, suddenly, I experienced the deepest chill that I had ever felt in my life.

"Do you feel that?" I asked my friend.

"Yes," she answered quickly. " It is freezing!"

We knew at once that we were feeling more than the cold from the river on this chilly autumn night. This was an otherworldly cold that chilled not only our bones, but also our hearts.

"I wonder what happened here?" she asked.

I was standing just inches in front of the calliope. The instrument was silent, yet something had cast an evil presence and it was trying to manifest itself. The coldness was starting to move up my legs and had reached my hips. As my eyes were drawn to the calliope, the coldness was making its way over my chest and was around my neck. The spirit made my speech difficult and my arms and legs felt weighed, as if movement wasn't possible any longer. As quickly as it tried to take possession of my body, it dissipated. My breathing returned to normal and I was able to move my arms and legs. The air returned to normal temperature and calmness was felt in the area around the calliope. But what the strange feeling was that associated or had attached itself to the calliope would remain a mystery for just a while longer. But we just knew that we were in the presence of something unexplained and that it made us uncomfortable. We immediately joined the others on the lower deck.

Downstairs, as the others compared stories of their own experiences, I slipped away from the group and caught the attention of one of the guides. I told him of my experience by the calliope. As I spoke, he dropped his gaze toward the floor and seemed to be staring at the polished wood. He simply nodded his head in agreement. I could tell that he knew something and he was preparing to speak.

"This happened," he said, "while the steamboat was the *Idelwild*. Two deckhands had gotten into an argument and it turned violent and bloody. As the accusations flew to one another, fists began flying. One of the deckhands had a knife on his person and stabbed the other guy to death. The murder occurred right by the calliope. You're not the only person to have sensed some form of coldness there and you won't be the last, either."

We had a few more minutes to continue exploring the Belle. It seems that we all went separate ways roaming about the steamboat, trying to imagine ourselves as one of the crewmembers from a different time period. I was no different from the others.

As the time passed, I found myself, along with a couple others, standing on one of the upper decks staring down at the red paddlewheel. The air was chilly, and I zipped up my jacket to shield me against the wind. The paddlewheel was motionless. Only a few drops of river water were dripping from the old wooden boards. The others, talking among themselves, moved on to another location. That left me standing alone.

One of the historians came up from behind, cleared his voice, and began to speak to me in a whispered tone.

"There is a tragic story that's supposed to be true about that paddlewheel," he said. "We don't know exactly when this happened but it was during the few short months that Captain Winters piloted this boat."

"I'd like to hear it," I told him.

"Well," he continued, "Captain Winters had a conflict with one of the crew members. They had quarreled quite a bit, and maybe it had something to do with the illegal activities of Captain Winters.

"There are different versions of what happened next, but we do know that the *Idlewild* was out of port and just floating in the river. It was late in the evening, yet it wasn't dark. Captain Winters saw an opportunity to end the conflict with the poor man forever, so he jumped on it. He noticed that his aggressor had positioned himself out on the paddlewheel to do a little maintenance. Some say that Captain Winters ordered the man to go out on the paddlewheel to do the work. In any event, the man was there and the captain put his wicked plan into action.

"Captain Winters went up to the pilothouse and gave the command to the engine room to fire up the boilers. Next, he bellowed out with the command of full steam ahead. He knew that the crewmember was on the paddlewheel. He was also aware that the paddlewheel would begin rotating.

"He mused to himself that it wouldn't take long, not long at all. Only seconds would be needed before the crewman would be chopped and churned to pieces. The trauma to the man's head would be enough, let alone drowning. In his mind, he could picture the crewman falling and hitting his head against the wooden boards. The roar of the engine would mask the groans and cries of the crewman. The only tell tale signs would be a stream of red, bloody water in the waves of the brown muddy river."

Does this evil deed prey on the mind of Captain Winters in the other world? Is that why many people claim to have seen his spectral form roaming on board the Belle of Louisville?

When I got home, I looked at the photographs I had taken inside the Captain's Quarters. I was startled to see a face looking at the camera from the wall. I squinted and looked again. There was no mistaking it. The face of a stern-looking man with a beard was staring from the picture, yet I was absolutely certain that nobody had been in that location when I took the photo.

I immediately e-mailed a copy of the picture to my friend who had been along on the tour. I did not make any comment about the man. I simply asked her to tell me what she saw in the picture.

"There's a face!" she replied.

She went on to describe the same face that I had seen but, at that time, neither of us knew the identity of the man I'd captured in the photograph.

Several days later, my friend came along on one of my Mr. Ghost Walker tours in downtown Louisville. As we walked along, she struck up a conversation with a young man who was also taking the tour. He mentioned that he was a former employee on the *Belle*.

"Really?" my friend asked. "Did you ever experience any paranormal happenings?"

"Oh, yes!" he replied.

"Our guide, Mr. Ghost Walker, took a picture in the Captain's Quarters..."

"Let me guess," the young man interrupted. "There was a face on the wall. It was a stern-looking man with a beard. That would be Captain Winters! He haunts the boat. Many people have seen him or captured his image in pictures."

"Does he haunt the upper deck?" she asked. "Mr. Ghost Walker and I had a chilling experience up there, but we didn't see anything."

When she related the experience, the young man didn't think that it was the captain's presence that we felt up there.

"Something did happen up there a long time ago, though," the young man admitted. "Two deckhands got into a fight and one killed the other."

When he pinpointed the location, it was the exact spot where we had been standing back in September on the tour. It was the same story that the guide told me that night.

My friend and I have both been back on the *Belle* numerous times, but we haven't had any other eerie experiences. My friend has gone searching in the Ladies Room for reflections of ghostly images reputed to show up sometimes in the mirrors there, but none made an appearance. I have taken many other pictures with my digital camera, but the ghostly captain has chosen not to pose again.

The *Belle of Louisville* disclaims all reports of paranormal activity, but those of us who have had these experiences believe otherwise. We like going back to see who or what might join us on another visit to The Belle.

3. UNSEEN HANDS ON THE CRADLE

The Brennan House
631 South Fifth Street

In 1868, just three years after the Civil War, an Italian-style, six-bedroom mansion was built on Fifth Street in residential Louisville. In 1884, Mr. Thomas Brennan, an inventor from Ireland, his wife, Mrs. Anna Bruce Brennan, from Cincinnati, Ohio, and their nine children came to call this house their home. He paid a sum of $15,000 for the property and moved into the stately home. Thanks to his family's efforts to fight the city and their steadfastness to preserve it against demolition, that home remains today as a memorial to a once grander lifestyle.

Out of the nine children, eight lived into adulthood. Thomas Munn Brennan died in infancy. Mrs. Brennan wrapped Thomas' tiny body into a burial cloth. Visitors soon began calling to view Thomas' body in the parlor of the house and to offer their condolences to the family. The same marble topped table that his body rested upon is still there. Of the eight children that lived into adulthood, five remained single and resided at the family property during their lives. Their absence was only brought about with times of travel to Europe or visits to other siblings who resided in New York City.

In 1908, at the age of 60, Mrs. Brennan's life came to an abrupt end. She died from complications of a broken hip. Her body was laid out in the front parlor for viewing upon her death so that friends and family could offer their condolences. Mr. Brennan was very distraught at the loss of his beloved wife. He would no longer sleep in the master bedroom that they had shared. He stopped eating his meals in the dining room and preferred solitude. Thomas Brennan died at the age of 75 and he willed this house to his youngest daughter, Beulah. She was unmarried and he wanted to provide for her.

In the parlor of the house are three portraits of Mr. and Mrs. Brennan hanging in a triangle position. The three paintings have been involved in some ghostly activity. At the top is a portrait of Mrs. Brennan, painted in the early years of the marriage. On the bottom left side is Mr. Brennan painted later in his married life, and on his right is Mrs. Brennan, painted later.

My interest in this magnificent link to the past has grown as I have taken tours and talked to the guides.

"On my mornings to open up the Brennan House for tours," the guide began, "I'd walk into the parlor and have to straighten up those three portraits of Mr. and Mrs. Brennan. Some mornings they are tilted to the left; other mornings they are tilted to the right; sometimes they are just hanging crooked without any pattern."

Guides have been puzzled by this strange phenomenon because the portraits of the daughters, Beulah and Mae, which also hang in the parlor, are always in perfect alignment.

Also in the parlor is a nine-foot grand piano that the girls used to play. The Brennans were very musical and enjoyed the cultural arts of the day. They could also play the violin. The girls treasured the grand piano so much that they took it with them when they traveled in Europe.

Dr. John practiced medicine from an office that he had built onto the northern side of the Brennan House in 1912. He was quite a character and was popular in the community. He never owned a vehicle but chose to walk or travel about town in a taxicab.

Rumor has it that when he'd make house call to his female patients, they'd open the door wearing the thinnest of sleepwear and would greet Dr. John with, "Oh doctor, I'm so glad you came."

Dr. John's library is adjacent to his medical office. A green colored Tiffany lamp is on his desk where he spent many hours pouring over medical books, all the while smoking cigars. Guides have told me that while they are preparing the house for visitors, they can smell the fragrance of cigars once they enter Dr. John's library. The mystery is that this is a smoke-free house and nobody could be smoking a cigar indoors, except for the ghost of Dr. John.

Upstairs in a simple nursery is a cradle that belonged to baby Napoleon. The nursery is adjacent to the master bedroom that was shared by Mr. and Mrs. Brennan. A doorway is between the two rooms and another doorway from the nursery leads into the hallway.

One long-time guide told me of a startling experience that left him both frightened and mystified!

"I had just finished my last tour of the day, and I had escorted the guests out the front door," began the elderly guide. "I've worked here a number of years, but I've never seen anything as strange as this. Eighteen steps lead to the

upstairs, and I had just reached the top when I heard the sound. It was like a clicky, click, clicky, click sound.

"From the top of the steps, I turned and looked down the hallway and I could clearly see inside the nursery. I walked gingerly down the hallway and stood in the doorway of the nursery. The cradle that belonged to Napoleon was rocking on its own. It was going hard, back and forth, back and forth and with so much force that the legs were being lifted off the ground. It scared me! There was no way that cradle could rock, no way, for the mechanical arm had been missing for decades.

"I turned and ran down the steps and began yelling for the other tour guide. She met me at the bottom of the steps, and I couldn't even get the words out I was so shaken up. The two of us went back upstairs and walked down the hallway. We just stood in the doorway and watched that cradle rock back and forth, back and forth. We both looked at each other, and never said a word, then we turned and watched that cradle. It started slowing down until it finally came to a rest on its own. It stopped. I remember that we just backed up a little and almost staggered back down the hallway, and never said a word as we turned."

"Do you know why that cradle rocked or anything about Napoleon's history?" I asked.

He cleared his throat and spoke, "When Napoleon was born, he had breathing problems. It brought him relief to have someone rock his cradle and that helped him breathe on his own. It must have been the motion."

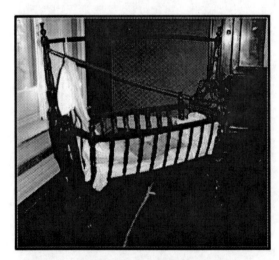

Napoleons Cradle at the Brennan House, which has a tendency to rock on its own.

"By any chance was his cradle rocking on his date of birth or possibly the anniversary of his death?"

"No, neither of those dates had anything to do with the cradle rocking. I've seen the cradle rocking on four separate occasions," he answered.

My research shows that Napoleon grew up and lived a normal life. He graduated from Centre College in Danville, worked for the FBI in Washington, DC, and later worked in the insurance business. He resided in the family home with his brothers and sisters.

Some homecomings were not so happy or productive. One of the sons, Thomas Brennan II, returned home to the family residence. Due to his suffering a stroke, it was his family who cared for him. He passed away in 1939 and other sad losses followed.

In 1948, death claimed brother Henry. The antiques he collected while traveling are still displayed in the house.

His sister, Beulah Bruce Brennan, passed away in 1952. No more piano or violin music would be heard from her hands.

In 1959, death came for the oldest of the Brennan family, Mae Bruce Brennan. She was known as the 'Beauty of Louisville' and she was recognized as a gifted pianist and multi-linguist of her day.

Dr. John's death came in 1963. He studied post-graduate medicine in Paris, France; Berlin, Germany; and London, England, and, while in Louisville, he had involvement with St. Anthony's Hospital.

One by one, Napoleon's siblings passed away and each one had their visitations and funerals in the parlor of the Brennan home. Little by little, the house grew more silent from their absence -- or did it? Did his brothers and sisters, who loved this property, actually leave? Or did they remain in spirit?

In 1963, when Napoleon was 77, he decided to marry. He brought home his new bride, a woman by the name of Opal. She was in the autumn season of her life, as well. She had a beautiful home in the Old Louisville neighborhood, just south of the downtown area and, for whatever the reason, she never left her home.

I've been told that on nights, as the newlywed couple lay sleeping in the master bedroom in the very same bed Mr. and Mrs. Brennan had once occupied, that Opal would be awoken during the night.

Rousing up in the bed, Opal would say, "Napoleon, did you hear that? It's the sound of piano music that I hear."

"Go back to sleep, Opal, you're dreaming," would be his response.

A few nights later, something similar would happen again.

"Napoleon, wake up! Don't you hear it?" she'd complain in a panic.

"Hear what?" he would say rousing from a deep sleep.

"Why, I hear violin music from downstairs," she stated.

The nights soon passed into weeks and the weeks into months. Opal kept hearing things or had visitations from family members who were still lingering in the house in spirit; piano music, then violin music; laughter echoed throughout the house; footsteps traveled up and down the stairwell; and someone walked about the third floor.

Opal was the first to exclaim, "This house is haunted and I'm not staying. You can go with me or you can remain in this haunted house."

And with that final statement, Opal packed her bags and retreated to her property in Old Louisville.

Napoleon found himself in a bad situation. He could stay in the family dwelling that he loved, or he could follow his wife to her home. Nobody knows how long Napoleon took to make his decision. But we do know this: he packed his bags, descended the 18 stairs with a heavy heart, closed the draperies, and locked the front doors forever.

Napoleon remained at his wife's property in Old Louisville for 14 years. Death came for him in 1977. He was 91 when he died. Opal outlived Napoleon by many years, for she died in February of 1997. Upon her death, she left behind an estate that exceeded five million dollars.

Questions still remain about who resides at the Brennan House. The evidence has been presented and you're free to draw your own conclusion.

On a recent ghost tour, one of the women lagged behind to ask me a question.

"Who did you have positioned upstairs to pass in front of the windows?" she asked. "Was that staged?"

Surprised, I said, "What do you mean? Did you see something?"

"Didn't you have somebody up there to scare us?" she persisted.

"Absolutely not!" I answered.

"At the end bedroom window, I saw someone pass with my own eyes. It was a good effect. It stood in the window, then moved over to the middle window and, finally, stood in the nursery window staring down at us," she elaborated.

"I assure you, I had nobody up there and this house is locked. I use no costumed characters at all," I answered her. "I do believe you. Maybe it was one of the Brennan family members looking down at us, wondering who the crowd was that had gathered on their front lawn."

On the tours, I look at that mansion where the past is so perfectly persevered and I wonder if somehow the Brennans are watching us. Because of their success in protecting the house against demolition, I can't help but feel that they have stayed on as proud hosts, welcoming those of us who care about the place as much as they did.

4. FOOTPRINTS IN THE DUST

The Brown Hotel
335 W. Broadway

On my downtown ghost walk, I have the guests stop at the statue of a man and a small dog.

"I'm so thankful that the artist who sculptured this likeness of Mr. Brown made him in this fashion. To glance at this statue, one might think that he is really here. And, from some accounts, it seems that he still is."

When I make that remark, I notice that people begin to glance over their shoulders and inch closer to me.

"This sculptured appearance is very accurate," I continue. "Mr. Brown stood at this height. He always was dressed wearing a suit and necktie, glasses, and often a hat while outdoors. Two things are missing, though. He was an avid cigar smoker, and there is no bottle of booze in his breast coat pocket."

At this point, I notice people staring at his coat pocket. Then I point to the little dog to draw their attention there.

"Mr. Brown loved his dog Woozem," I tell the crowd. "He rescued Woozem

(Right) The statue of Mr. James Graham Brown — and his faithful dog Woozem — outside of the Brown Hotel.

from abandonment. The circus was lodging at the hotel during the 1940s, and they no longer had any need for the dog act that Woozem delivered to the audience. The circus planned on leaving Woozem on the street, but Mr. Brown had fallen in love with him and, in today's terms, he adopted this poodle. Woozem lived in the lap of luxury, complete with a specially designed and crafted highchair, sterling silver bowls for eating and water consumption, and sterling silver serving spoons."

People were looking at the statue of Mr. Brown and Woozem as if they both were still alive. Woozem could very well be alive -- at least in spirit.

Guests and employees of the hotel have spoken of hearing the barks of a small dog in the lobby.

"I was enjoying a cocktail on the second floor lobby not too long ago, and I heard the sound of a dog barking. Being a dog lover, I stood and looked around but I saw no dog. I just assumed that it was a dog outdoors. I casually pulled back the drapery and looked down, and what caught my eye was the statue of the dog next to Mr. Brown's statue. I couldn't help but laugh at myself for thinking that I'd heard a dog barking in the hotel," a guest said.

An employee had a little more to add to the topic.

"In a back area for employees only, I know that I've heard the sound of a dog running on the tile floor. And I've also heard a dog scratching on the back doors of the rooms. I'd look around and wonder to myself how did a dog get back here, and I've never seen a dog at all. But I've sure heard the dog," he added.

The Brown Hotel is one of Louisville's most treasured landmarks. It opened for business on October 25, 1923. This corner has been known over the decades as the Magic Corner. Great things have happened here. The famous Kentucky Hot Brown sandwich was birthed here in 1925 as his signature dish. WAVE radio first began broadcasting here and had studios on the 15th floor. And much sorrow has been experienced here, as well. The 1937 floodwaters submerged three to four feet of the lobby, but it survived.

World War II and the financial hardships faced by our country impacted the hotel industry. The day came when the hotel's doors were locked and the glorious windows were boarded up forever.

Yet, one identity remained on the property. That identity has roamed the desolate lobby and ballrooms of this once grand hotel, and that is the ghost of Mr. James Graham Brown.

Mr. Brown was born in 1881, so this hotel was his home until 1969 when he died at the age of 88. He owned land in the city, but he called this hotel his home.

"I feel like Mr. Brown resided upon the 15th floor of the hotel," recited a hotel historian who has been involved here for years. "I also feel like the ghost of Mr.

James Graham Brown haunts the 15th floor."

Other hotel employees share the same opinion.

Hosting the ghost walking tours have provided me with wonderful opportunities to get to know employees of these buildings along the route. One such man is Justin, a doorman at the Brown Hotel. Justin greets us out front. He is dressed in a spotless white uniform shirt with brass buttons down the front. His black pants are lint free and he is wearing black sneakers. Mr. Brown would be pleased with Justin's performance as well as the other doormen who are the first to greet the guests at the hotel. He welcomes us by opening the door for the walkers and me as I lead into the lobby.

"I've worked the second shift at this hotel for several years now," he said. "There is something creepy about going to the 15th floor to get items for the hotel. Nobody goes up there alone. The 15th floor is completely gutted from end to end. Plastic covers the floor; the windows are dirty which limits natural light. Mattresses are stacked higher than your head, so being able to see around corners is difficult. Plaster from the ceiling is falling and everything is covered with a white chalky dust.

Justin — doorman at the Brown Hotel

"I remember this well. Another buddy and I had to go up there once to get something for a meeting. We stepped off the elevator and started meandering around the stacks of chairs, mattresses, lamps, and the round banquet tables. As luck would have it, we stayed together and never separated.

"The bell from the elevator sounded, and we could hear the doors opening. My buddy and I looked up together, trying to peer over the mattresses. We were standing near the Broadway end of the building, and we both called out to see who had gotten off the elevator. Nobody answered.

"As we stood there in silence facing each other, we could hear a shuffling of heavy feet against the plastic. We called out again, 'Who's there?' There was no reply.

Something, or someone, was walking our way. Whoever was, they were not replying.

"My heart started racing! The sound was coming closer and nobody identified themselves. We just started making our way back toward the elevator, totally forgetting about our purpose there, and planning on escaping whomever was up there.

The famous Brown Hotel in downtown Louisville

"We never saw the person who had exited the elevator, but we did notice something rather strange and puzzling. As I mentioned, gray plastic covers the flooring and everything is layered with heavy plaster dust. While waiting for the elevator to arrive, we both looked down and noticed the prints from the sneakers we were wearing in the dust. I was wearing Converse Chuck Taylor sneakers, which has a unique diamond crisscross pattern, and my friend had on Nikes, which has a zigzag sole print. We could plainly see the prints from our own sneakers; however, we also noticed an additional set of footprints. A man, or something, exited the elevator wearing hard sole shoes for we saw a total of three sets of footprints in the dust on the plastic. We decided not to follow the third set of footprints and let whoever was up there just remain."

Other employees encountered evidence that there is ghostly activity at the Brown. One lady at the front desk was helping a guest check out. This is her story.

"I've worked as a reservation clerk here at the hotel for several years," she began. "A young woman was checking out of her room on the 14th floor. I asked her how she enjoyed her stay at the Brown Hotel and made some casual small talk about the history of the hotel. Her countenance changed.

"She told me that she didn't sleep a wink and began complaining about the guests who were in the room above her on the 15th floor.

"I made notes as she spoke so that I could pass the information on to the general manager. We needed to investigate because no guests are on the 15th floor. She began to tell about the heavy footsteps that she heard, and the sounds of things being pulled or pushed across the floor.

"Once she finished, I offered my apologies for her restless night of sleep. I passed the information on to the general manager. He and another man went up to investigate and they navigated their way to an area so that they'd be over her room on the 14th floor.

"Checking out the area looking at mattresses and chairs or expecting to see something that had toppled over, those men found nothing out of the ordinary. They simply passed off the noises and disturbances she had heard as being the activity of Mr. Brown."

However, Mr. Brown does not confine his activity to the 15th floor. He sometimes makes his presence known in the kitchen.

The hotel also offers its guests plenty of opportunity to dine in historic excellence. The kitchen staff is made up of many people who report to work to prepare for breakfast while the rest of the guests sleep peacefully in their beds.

"I've been preparing breakfast at the hotel for a long time," said an older lady wearing her white uniform. "I usually arrive around 4:30 AM. I'm known for my wonderful biscuits that I fix here.

"One morning, I was working at the counter getting the ingredients ready for the homemade biscuits. Just across the kitchen is the service elevator. The kitchen was particularly quiet that morning and that bell from the service elevator really sounded loud. I looked up and noticed that the light for floor 15 was lit.

"I stopped what I was doing, wondering who was traveling on the service elevator at that hour of the morning. I watched as the light from the 15th floor lit up, all the way down to the ground floor. I couldn't help but be curious. I looked around and I didn't see any other employees nearby. Then, those doors opened but nobody got off.

"I just stood there, shrugged my shoulders and went back to the biscuits. It wasn't but one minute later when the bell rang again and I saw those elevator doors open wide. That really did surprise me. The doors closed and that elevator started traveling back up into the building. My eyes followed the lights of each floor and I just watched each floor light up until it reached the 15th.

"I was told later that morning, when I mentioned it to another employee, that Mr. Brown used to ride the service elevator in the morning and come down to the kitchen for a cup of coffee. Then he'd go back up to his apartment. Well, that wasn't the last time that I'd witnessed that elevator traveling from the 15th floor down here to the kitchen."

Is Mr. Brown still keeping a close eye on all the hotel's operations? Nobody knows for sure, but his apparition has also been seen on the mezzanine level. The historians believe that Mr. Brown conducted his business from the corner suites in this area. Beautifully stenciled golden arches grace the mezzanine level and offer a panoramic view of the lobby and all activity. Mr. Brown's apparition has been seen standing in the arch.

"During very busy times, such as conventions or Derby, the apparition of Mr. Brown has manifested itself. His posture is quite intimidating and startling. He'll be leaning forward with his hands grasping that wooden railing, one foot placed slightly behind, and in his mouth would be a stubby little cigar. His eyes would be staring down as if keeping an eye on the employees to keep them honest," the historian stated. "Then, I'd blink my eyes and the apparition would be gone. On occasion, I've raced up those stairs to the mezzanine level to stand in that arch. And you know what? I've sniffed the aroma of a cigar from that arch! What is eerie is that this is a smoke-free building."

The questions remain the same after all these years and the answers are still as mysterious. Is Mr. Brown haunting his own hotel? Nobody knows for sure, but you're free to draw your own conclusions.

5. A STARTLING STAGE PRESENCE

The Brown Theater
315 West Broadway

Sometimes things that happen behind the scenes are as intriguing as those that happen on stage. This could be said of the activity at the Brown Theater on Broadway. There are those who have experienced action not called for by a director, and they have experienced sights and sounds not produced by any actors or backstage crews! Those who have experienced the eerie phenomena do not know the reason.

Some say that departed spirits are disturbed when places that they loved are changed or remodeled. If that is true, then maybe some spirits are drawn to the Brown Theater, which has had its share of changes.

The theater, located at 315 W. Broadway, was built in 1925 by J. Graham Brown. This theater replaced the old Macauley, which was demolished that year.

Just five years later, in 1930, the Brown was wired for talkies to be shown in the 1,500-seat auditorium. The theater was remodeled in 1962, and live performances were returned to the stage.

During live performances, stagehands are needed for the operation of the production. Several of these stagehands were witnesses to strange occurrences that they could not explain and they were willing to share them with me.

Many of these experiences happened when the stagehands were working in the Green Room located below the stage. On occasions when only a few workers were present and most of the stage area was deserted, workers heard footsteps walking about on the stage above them.

Knowing full well that the lights were out and the stage was empty, the stagehands listened in amazement to the footsteps crossing stage left and stage right, just walking back and forth as if a performance or rehearsal were in progress! Curiosity getting the best of the workers, they went upstairs to investigate. Their findings left a little spark of fear that ignited along their spines and crept into their minds. Nobody was on stage! All the lights were out and the curtains were closed. So who or what had been walking overhead while they were working? Was it possible that all of them had imagined the whole thing? They didn't think that was very likely.

Three workers that I contacted agreed to meet with me to relate things that they had experienced.

On this particular day, I met with three employees representing Axxis Lighting and Sound, two men and one woman. It looked like it would take more than a few ghosts to disturb this crew of workers, but I have learned that each person has their own tolerance for the paranormal.

All three looked like normal, competent workers. Both men were large, muscular guys dressed in denim jeans, work boots, and company owned white shirts. The woman had on jeans and a polo top.

Stepping just inside of the lobby of the theater, each person seemed eager to tell me about some unexplained personal experience.

The woman spoke of her experience first:

"I've worked at this theater for a number of years and I'm familiar with all of the quirks about the building, both up in the balcony and down on stage. So I recognize the unusual immediately.

"I was working a show one night and everything was going smoothly. We had spotlights up in the balcony, and it was my job to follow the guest performers on stage with my spotlight. Overhead, we had some scaffolding set up for additional lighting on the stage. The theater was dark with the exception of the stage lighting and my spotlight on the actor.

"From the corner of my eye, I started to see a figure climbing about on the scaffolding. I knew that couldn't be happening! I was able to pause long enough with the spotlight to watch and try to figure out what was going on. I watched, mystified, as the figure reached the top.

"It was white or gray in color, and its shape was ever changing. I could see legs and arms and what looked like a flowing gown. Then the figure would transform into something like a cloud. Next, it would reshape again with legs and arms.

"Watching it move across the scaffolding, I concluded that it must be female. It didn't look large enough to be male. As she moved, I could almost see through her even though she had a cloud-like appearance, almost like a mist. Once she reached the opposite end, she simply faded from my sight. I never saw her again."

We all exchanged glances and I could tell that everybody was serious. The woman seemed shaken just remembering the experience. She was not making up the story.

Then one of the men began to speak.

"This wasn't too long ago, so it's not ancient history. The two of us had been working on stage and making sure that everything was all set up for an evening performance. We turned out all the stage lights and locked all stage doors. Then we went downstairs to the Green Room to finalize everything and discuss the plan of the show one last time.

"As we tried to relax and go over the plan, we were suddenly disturbed by the sound of dancing, something like tap dancing, overhead. The sound was very distinct since the stage was right overhead. We stopped and looked at each other, wondering who might be up there dancing on the floor. We tried to ignore it but it continued. Our curiosity got the best of us so we decided to go up and check it out.

"We left the Green Room and climbed a back staircase to reach the stage. We found the door still locked and, once we unlocked it and stepped inside, the area was completely dark. As we moved about backstage, we could clearly hear tap dancing. It was unbelievable that anyone would be dancing in total darkness, but there was no mistaking the sound. I yanked back a stage curtain while my buddy here flipped on the switch. The stage was lit up immediately and we just stood there, motionless, neither of us believing our eyes! Nobody was there!"

The other man nodded his corroboration.

"That's right," he said,. "We just stood there in disbelief! We know what we heard, but nobody was scrambling off that stage!"

"We tried to reason it out," the first man continued. "We thought that maybe we were too tired to be rational or that we heard outside noises, but we knew that wasn't true. We were not imagining the noises that we had heard on stage.

"We went back to the Green Room to continue our work. But no sooner had we entered the room and sat down when we heard the same noise overhead again: tap, tap, and tap! Whoever it was was back! It had to be someone playing a prank.

"This time we formed a plan. One of us would go up the left side while the other went up on the right side. We'd use our phones as a signal to enter at the same time. My buddy here would flip on the lights and I would rush the stage. That way, we'd catch the practical joker once and for all."

"Yes," said the second guy. "We stood backstage in a hallway with everything set. I thought 'this is going to be fun'.

"We signaled," the first man continued, "and we unlocked the doors. I raced onto the stage, parting the curtains and dodging props like mad. He flipped on the lights, which almost blinded me with the intensity. We both ended up facing each other on the stage with the curtains billowing behind us. Nobody was present and there was no sign that anyone had ever been there. Nothing had been disturbed. No props had been moved.

"We decided to take a break and let whoever wanted to practice their dance steps have the stage."

"We had another encounter with a ghost, though," said the second man. "It happened one afternoon last summer. He and I were standing in center stage, facing the empty seats in the theater. We both were holding clipboards and double-checking all the placement of the spotlights. We heard footsteps come up from behind us, but neither of us paused or stopped long enough to turn around.

"Excuse me," said a man with a British accent. 'What's playing here tonight?'

"Neither of us turned to address the man, but I did respond. 'The Louisville Ballet will be here tonight at 8 PM.'

"We were still focused on the lighting of the scaffolding.

'Thank you very much,' our British visitor said.

"At that moment, we both turned to see who had spoken. Nobody was standing there, but we could clearly hear his footsteps going across the stage away from us. But if that wasn't eerie enough, once the ghost reached the back curtains, he evidently took his hand and reached out and parted the curtains so he could pass. The curtain just dropped back into place and had a slight ripple until it came to a stop.

"I had never seen anything like it before, and I sure hope that I don't see anything like it again soon."

So the shows go on. If you are in the audience, you may have to decide for yourself if all the action is from the script, or if some of the characters you see in the wings are from a stage with its own invisible curtain.

6. THE GHOSTLY BAG LADY

Cathedral of the Assumption
443 South Fifth Street

Since I began conducting the Louisville Ghost Walks, I have been constantly on the look out for new, haunted sites and stories. My research has revealed that quite a few people have had unexplained experiences in the downtown area that they are eager and willing to talk about.

One site that kept showing up in my research was the Cathedral of the Assumption located at 443 South Fifth Street.

The cathedral is quite an impressive Gothic structure, making a focal point for the downtown skyline with its spiraling clock tower. Going back to 1805, St. Louis Catholic was the first church to occupy that location. The neighborhood changed and a second church was in that location from 1830 to 1841; eventually, it progressed from a church to a cathedral. It's been anchoring that section of south Fifth Street since 1852. It is the seat of the Roman Catholic Archdiocese of Louisville.

In the undercroft beneath the altar is the remains of Benedict Joseph Flaget, but his spirit is not the one believed to roam the sanctuary. The reports I received were about another ghostly apparition that attends services at the church.

At first, I had trouble finding a witness to any ghostly visitations but, eventually, I was fortunate enough to meet someone who could give me a first-hand account. He had heard about me though the publicity about the Louisville Ghost Walks. The gentleman who identified himself as Tim contacted me to share a strange experience that he had at the Cathedral of the Assumption.

I agreed to meet with Tim at a restaurant on Bardstown Road so that I could hear his story. All I knew was his first name and a brief description of how he would be dressed.

"I have dark hair," he told me, "and I'll be wearing a green colored sports coat and glasses."

That description would fit any number of men in the city so I didn't know what to expect. As it turned out, the meeting went off without a hitch. I was pleased to find Tim to be a pleasant young man who seemed to have been a credible witness to a paranormal happening in the cathedral.

"I'm not Catholic by faith," Tim began, "but I find the worship meaningful to my spirit."

"I understand," I told him. "The cathedral attracts people of many faiths."

"An early morning mass occurs during the week. When I attend, I usually sit near the rear of the church.

"On this particular September morning, I arrived a few minutes late and the service was already in progress. It seemed like fewer than 20 people were in the congregation that morning and most had taken seats near the front.

"The priest had invited everyone who desired the Eucharist to come forward. Since I don't receive Holy Communion, I remained seated with my head bowed in prayer and reverence."

He paused and then looked at me. I nodded my understanding so he took a deep breath and went on.

"My thoughts and prayers were soon disturbed by excessive amounts of noise from a latecomer. I raised my head just a little and, using my peripheral vision, I saw the two double doors open just enough to allow someone to enter."

"Could you see who it was?" I asked.

"That's the odd thing," he answered. "I saw nobody! When I glanced over my shoulder, nobody was there."

"Then what happened?" I asked him. "What did you do?"

"I lowered my head once again," he said. "Then I heard a low roar start, like the sound of wind blowing. It created an eerie tone. A chilly draft of air blew around my feet, and I could hear distinct footsteps shuffling along on the marble floor."

"That's weird," I said.

"That's not all," he added. "Whoever it was must have been carrying shopping bags I thought, the paper kind, because I heard them scruntch and crunch together. Even with my head still bowed down, I could hear someone very plainly making his or her way down the aisle near me. The pew in that aisle creaked and moaned as something unseen began moving between the rows, as if in preparation to take a seat. Frankly, I was getting a little annoyed at this individual. I was curious to see how the rest of the congregation was reacting to this intrusion. I raised my head, opened my eyes, and looked forward.

"To my surprise, several of the parishioners were staring back at me with mean glares. Apparently, the sounds that I heard echoed so badly that it disturbed their worship service, but there was more to it than that. I could see they assumed that I was the one responsible for the disturbance but I wasn't! The church was silent and I could feel their icy stares."

"Oh, no!" I sympathized. "What did you do?"

"I glanced around, trying to detract their attention from me to the guilty party who was seated opposite of me. I turned, looked, and expected to see some individual sitting on the pew. To my surprise, I saw that all the pews, one after another, were empty! There was not a soul in sight. I bowed my head again and hurried out when the service ended."

"What do you think it was?" I asked.

"I don't know," he said. "Maybe some bag lady came inside to rest and pray. I can't explain it at all, but I know what I heard and felt."

Stories like Tim's persist but, so far, the invisible visitor remains unknown.

7. THE MOURNFUL MARRIAGE CEREMONY

Henry Vogt / Doe Anderson Mansion
223 East Broadway

Some believe that there are places that hold spirits earthbound. These spirits, or ghosts, may remain here for any number of reasons such as love, hate, unfinished business, or because a sudden, violent death takes them so quickly that they do not realize that they are dead. Even though science has no concrete proof that souls linger after death, there is evidence of paranormal sightings by reliable witnesses that can't be written off to imagination.

An old mansion located in downtown Louisville is one of these places where many spirits remain and have been encountered by the living. The witnesses to those apparitions know that those spirits are connected to this old house.

This mansion that was built in the late 1800s stands today as a memorial to wealth, industrialization, and to the spirit of one man's entrepreneurial lifestyle. Henry Vogt designed this property at 223 East Broadway in downtown Louisville. The three-story, Tudor-style mansion became his home.

The mansion has seen its fair share of parties, receptions, and other joyful occasions over the years. That same house has also known the dark shadows of suicide. Sadly, the victim who found no peace among the living has yet to find peace among the dead.

In my search and interviews, I came across "skeleton stories" not fully "fleshed out" by the tellers, but these ghostly glimpses give lasting impressions of life's continuity between this world and the next.

Many people have come and gone through the front doors of the mansion. Some were residents, some were invited guests, and others came to conduct business in the building.

Some of those people have attachments to the mansion and have never left. Their spirits ascend and descend the main stairwell; heartache and tragedy still

haunt an upstairs bedroom; voices are heard in both the afternoon and evening hours; and there are sudden drops in the temperature of rooms. Something ominous occurred in the mansion in another time period that affected those individuals for eternity.

My search for the poor souls who are referred to as ghosts in this story led me to tenants of the not-so-distant past.

In 1972, Doe Anderson Advertising Agency acquired the property form the Lemmon and Sons Gallery, which was a jewelry business. The property became the main headquarters for many years until Doe Anderson relocated on West Main Street. Doe Anderson conducts its business there today.

Currently, the East Broadway property has been purchased by a local hospital for their private usage.

It was from the occupancy of the Doe Anderson Advertising Agency that I gained the most information in my research. Several employees had strange experiences that they couldn't explain and they were willing to grant me interviews.

"Not a single day has passed that some kind of weird or strange phenomenon is not told by the workers in the old mansion," stated Bob, a long time employee of the agency.

"That's right," remarked Jim, a pleasant gentleman with graying hair which seemed to make him an unlikely subject for a spooky story.

"Are you telling me that you experienced paranormal activity yourself?" I inquired.

Jim nodded his head in answer to my question.

"I worked for the Doe Anderson Advertising firm for many years," he said. "In fact, I was in that house for 17 years and I witnessed first-hand all kinds of strange and startling activities that just couldn't be explained."

"Give me an example," I requested.

"Well," he said, "this one still gives me chills when I think about it. In my corner office on the second floor around five o'clock each day during one autumn season, an unseen hand would unlock the latch and the window would rise up a few inches all by itself. Nobody was near the window. There was no way that this could happen of its own accord."

He shivered involuntarily as he finished speaking.

"That would give me chills, too!" I agreed. "Did you ever come up with a logical explanation?"

"I don't know if I actually found an explanation," Jim answered, "but I did come up with an interesting possibility.

"My curiosity just got the best of me, so I decided to do a little research on the Vogt family. History has revealed to us some challenging pieces of information about this mansion.

"When the Vogts lived here, they hosted a lavish reception for a wedding party. Everybody who was anybody was present. Unfortunately, a jilted lover approached the bride with some troubling news about a previous relationship that she had with the groom. Those who were present witnessed the disturbing confrontation as the two exchanged fiery words and glances.

"A sudden hush fell on the guests. All eyes were on the bride and her rival. The young bride rushed up the stairs to a bedroom of the house as her adversary stormed out the front door. The guests stood in disbelief as to what they had heard and seen between the two women.

"Then abruptly, before they could recover, the guests heard gunshots from an upstairs room. They hurried up the steps and discovered a ghastly sight. The young bride had committed suicide. The carpet began soaking up her blood as she lay sprawled across the floor. The white bridal gown she was wearing was forever ruined, as well as her hope for marital happiness. Nothing could be done. She was dead.

"Those who attended the internment said that the poor girl was laid out in her coffin wearing a pair of white wedding gloves. Clasped in her hands was her bridal veil. It seemed apparent that the young maiden was taking that veil with her to her grave."

"How sad," I commented.

"Yes," said Jim, as he stood up and walked to the window. "I believe that she still haunts the mansion. Maybe raising my window was her way of letting me know about her presence."

"Something definitely is here," agreed Bryan, a middle-aged guy wearing Levi jeans and a plaid shirt. "At least, I think so."

"Why?" I asked. "Did you experience something, too?"

"Yes," he answered me. "Lots of times!"

"Like what?" I asked him.

"There were several things that made a believer out of me," he replied. "I worked at Doe for a long time and it wasn't anytime at all before I started hearing voices in the mansion, like a party was going on. It would echo up the stairs. And it would be so intense that I would wonder who was hosting a party here.

"On some occasions, I would clearly hear footsteps ascending and descending the hall stairs. The boards would creak as if someone heavy was on them. I'd glance out and look down the hall, but there was nobody to be seen.

"I could hear sounds of laughter and glasses tinkling together, as if being raised for a toast. Voices of light conversations drifted to my ears. Soon a loud scream and cries would follow. That was the most unsettling to me, hearing the screams and sobs of people crying.

"When I first heard the scream and the crying sounds, it scared me so bad that I fled from my office that night. I jumped over a banister and landed on the staircase. From there, I flew down the steps and right out the front door. I don't even recall locking the front door of the mansion. I just wanted to leave!"

"Do you think that you were hearing the wedding party that ended in the bride's suicide?" I asked.

"I don't know," he said, "but the things I heard seem to correspond to the happenings at that tragic event."

The last employee I interviewed was a man named Norman.

"I had an experience that made me know a woman is here," he said. "Who knows? Maybe I met the bride."

"What happened?" I prompted him.

"It was like this," he said. "One evening the hour was late and I knew that I was alone in the building. My office was on the third floor, in one of the former bedrooms when the mansion was used as an estate. I was descending the stairs and reached the landing on the second floor. I had just turned off the light so the third floor was totally dark. As I walked down the hallway, I heard a female voice call from a dark office.

" 'Good night, Norman!'

'Well, that surprised me. I knew that I was alone in the building and I didn't recognize her voice. I stepped to the threshold of the room where the voice originated and stopped. I placed my hand on the wall and moved it along until I found the light switch. I flipped on the light, expecting to see a co-worker with a sly grin on her face. That was not the case. To my surprise, there was nobody in the room.

"It occurred to me that the woman might be hiding, so I quietly stepped around to the back of the desk and placed my hand on the chair. I was thinking to myself that I was about to expose a practical joker. I yanked out the chair and bent down, expecting to see someone crouched under the desk. I couldn't believe my eyes. Nobody was there. I felt a bit foolish as I stood up and slid the chair back under the desk.

"As I hurried from the room, I began to question my own reasoning ability and my own sense of hearing. But I knew what I heard. A female voice had called me by name and told me goodnight! I decided not to search the property any further and allow whomever voiced that goodnight to me remain a secret!"

The old mansion may never reveal its secrets, but other employees confirm the ghostly party of ghosts. Are they members of the ill-fated wedding party, or are they ghostly guests at other parties, just trying to recapture those last minutes of a happier time in the mansion?

For now, I've decided to follow Norman's lead and search no farther. But that may change in the future if these ghostly inhabitants make further contact with the living.

8 TWO SPIRITS FROM THE PAST

The Holiday Inn
120 West Broadway

The Holiday Inn at the corner of Second and Broadway in downtown Louisville hardly looks like it would have a ghost or two roaming the halls. The red brick building with typical 1960s architecture is not old by any standards, yet it occupies a very important place in Louisville's haunted past.

Our story begins not at Second and Broadway but on Main Street, several blocks north of Broadway. The main character in this part of the story is Horatio Dalton Newcomb, or H.D. Newcomb. Newcomb was not a Louisvillian by birth. He hailed from Springfield, Massachusetts, and was born on August 10, 1809. For unknown reasons, Newcomb made his way to Louisville in 1832.

Newcomb was pursuing a livelihood in retail, and his fixation was on selling furs and pelts. He was a natural born salesman and it wasn't long until he had established himself in the community not only as a leader, but also as one of the wealthiest men in Louisville. As his business ventures matured and changed directions, Newcomb found himself making a profitable living in the liquor business. Keeping up with his prominent lifestyle, he built a mansion on Main Street that was between Brook and First Streets. In 1837, he and his brother merged their assets and opened a grocery distribution which they ran for a number of years. Their specialty was molasses, sugar, and coffee. Soon, the grocery business gave way to the liquor industry once again. Life was good but it was getting ready to take a serious turn and change Newcomb's life forever.

On June 23, 1838, Newcomb married a woman by the name of Cornelia Read and they had four children. While it may have appeared to be the perfect family, it wasn't long before their marital bliss started spiraling out of control. Over the years of their brief marriage, Cornelia became unstable and her mental condition deteriorated. This led to one of Louisville's most tragic happenings. One day, while sitting with her young children by an upper floor window in the

Main Street mansion, Cornelia perceived that God had sent her a message. She did not hesitate to obey. She threw the four children from the upper floor window! Only two survived the fall. Two died upon impact.

Police joined the neighbors at the grisly scene. Doctors provided all of the help possible for the two surviving children. Police and H. D. Newcomb led Mrs. Newcomb from the mansion that day. Court officials began an inquest into Cornelia's mental condition. She stated that God called for the children and she was simply following His directive by sending them to Him. It wasn't long before Cornelia was declared insane. Newcomb had her placed in the Massachusetts General Hospital For The Insane near Boston and tried to pick up the pieces of his broken life.

Trying to live a normal life with the two surviving children was not easy. The image of that dreadful day just kept playing over and over in his mind and the minds of his children. Realizing that life would never be the same, Newcomb knew that he needed to start over somewhere else. He purchased a tract of property on Broadway, between First and Second Streets, and built a mansion larger and more beautiful than the one before. It had two floors and many rooms, including a ballroom. In 1859, the remaining Newcombs moved away from the old house of death to the new place where joy would be restored to the family.

In early 1871, the state of Kentucky allowed divorces to be granted on the grounds of insanity. Newcomb then filed for divorce from Cornelia Read. After a whirlwind courtship from March to December of that same year, Newcomb, aged 61, wed Mary C. Smith.

The second Newcomb family enjoyed a grand lifestyle in the mansion on Broadway. With a limestone façade and columns on the front, the house stood three stories tall with a circular driveway that extended to the front. The western side of the mansion had two sets of bay windows on the first and second floors, which would have invited guests to enjoy the panoramic view of the lawn and the greenhouse in the back corner lot. Lavish parties and dances were the norm in the Newcomb house, and social gatherings attracted wealthy from all parts of the city. Newcomb was known and had lots of associates throughout the city because of his career with the railroad. Mary evidently excelled as a hostess and enjoyed that role. The mansion was rarely void of dances, and the glow of lights burned brightly.

At age 62, Newcomb fathered his first son with Mary. The next year, they had a second son. Newcomb's joy was not to last, though. He did not live long enough to see his sons reach manhood. He died of a stroke in his beloved mansion on August 18, 1874, at the age of 65. Mrs. Mary Newcomb continued living an elegant lifestyle in the home for several more years. Perhaps it was her

role as hostess that eased the pain of her loss and kept her going with memories of happy days when her husband was alive.

As Mary Newcomb advanced in age, decisions were made for preservation of the property that she and her late-husband cherished. In 1890, the mansion housed an exclusive female seminary known at Miss Annie Nold's School. Unfortunately, Miss Nold's school didn't last long. The following year, 1892, the Xaverian brothers leased the home. It became St. Xavier College and was established for the education and moral development for Catholic males of Irish and German immigrants. Over the next nine years, the school continued to grow in popularity. It was soon announced that the Newcomb estate at 118 W. Broadway had been sold to St. Xavier. In 1901, the original Newcomb property was demolished for the expansion of the school.

The Holiday Inn now stands on the former Newcomb estate. In front of the hotel is a white wrought iron fence. It is the only trace of the grand mansion from Newcomb's time that remains today. Or is it?

When I began investigating sites for the Louisville Ghost Walks, I heard from a former employee of the Holiday Inn that other things from the past might remain at this location. There were stories that a lady in an old-fashioned gown was seen by several people waltzing in the ballroom on the 12th floor. An assistant investigator and I went to the Holiday Inn to check out the stories. The staff was very cooperative and allowed us access to the haunted site.

Along with the hotel security guard, we boarded the elevator. Even though he seemed a bit uncomfortable talking about ghosts, he was willing to share what information he had.

"I've worked here about six months," he said. "It wasn't any time until I started hearing the stories about the Waltzing Woman up on the 12th floor. I haven't seen her, but I have to admit that there is something about securing the 12th floor late at night that is creepy. I'm 6'2" and not really scared of anyone, but I feel really uneasy up there."

Stepping off of the elevator, we had to pass through two sets of frosted glass doors that were bolted. I couldn't help but notice the security of this ballroom and how difficult it would be to gain access here. It would be almost impossible for any living person to get inside and dance without permission.

Our guide led us past the bar, which is on one side of the ballroom. Windows are on all three sides revealing the city of Louisville with views of the west, north, and east. Mirrored columns were arranged about the ballroom, which reflected our own images.

"I've heard several employees say," our guide continued, "that the lady they see dancing around this dance floor has a gray-like appearance. Her arms are positioned as if she is holding a partner. Nobody has seen her face as she moves about. They say that she is wearing a long dancing gown which isn't from the time period of our life. It's old-fashioned clothing. When people approach her, she simply fades from view. She hasn't ever made contact with anyone."

We wandered around the empty circular tables and passed chairs scattered in disarray. Our guide leaned against one of the mirrored columns, dropped his hands into his pockets, and continued to recount what he had heard.

"Custodial workers have reported that they hear footsteps on the wooden floor. These guys have seen the spirit of a woman waltzing on the dance floor, but I haven't. That doesn't mean she doesn't exist. I think that something is here, I just don't know what."

Whoever she is or what connection she has with the ballroom is a mystery. With each turn of her waltz, she slips further away into obscurity. But one possible connection exists. Could this apparition be the ghost of the late Mary Newcomb? Could the hotel guests draw her back to a time when she was a gracious hostess for guests of her own? Does she think the hotel ballroom is the ballroom in her mansion where she and her husband danced in happier times?

While the identity of the ghostly, dancing woman remains unknown, another lady who haunts the Holiday Inn can readily be identified. Instead of being sociable, Marys Converse spent most of her time behind locked doors, fearful that her life was in danger.

"Every now and then," an older housekeeper began to explain, "when a guest sees me in the hallway, the first question that they ask is if I came into their room and closed the draperies, or if I opened or closed the closet door or the bathroom door. My answer is always the same, 'No, it wasn't me.' Of course, they look puzzled and tell me that someone did those things during the evening or nighttime. Sometimes, guests will tell me that they smell White Castle hamburgers in the room. I can't help but laugh. I'll just look them in the eye and tell them, 'It's simply the ghost of Miss Marys.' Then their eyes get real big, but I reassure them by telling them that Miss Marys won't hurt them at all."

"I've worked here since 1981 and she lived here then," Liz, the front desk clerk, told me. She continued, "I don't know when Miss Marys moved into the hotel, but money wasn't an object. I know that she was eccentric and lived a reclusive life with a private nurse and bodyguards 24 hours a day."

Miss Marys Converse was the daughter of Marquis Converse of Massachusetts. Her wealth came from the Converse All-Star Athletic Shoe Company founded by her father and Charles Goodyear. Miss Marys resided in Louisville, Kentucky, because she was the owner and publisher of a family newspaper, The Christian Observer. And why Miss Marys haunts the second floor remains a mystery to this day.

Miss Marys gets blamed for lots of unusual happenings on the third floor, from the service elevator's constant activity when no passengers are on board, window draperies being closed, and doors being found open or closed for no apparent reason. Miss Marys occupied the entire third floor of the hotel, which consisted of 17 rooms. When she moved into the hotel, the room rate was $29 per day, and she rented all 17 rooms on the third floor. During the course of her ailing life span, the rooms she rented decreased down to only the rooms on the western side of the hotel along Second Street and, eventually, down to just two or three rooms. Hotel records show that her room rate remained constant at $29 per day until the day she died.

"I remember this about Miss Marys," added Liz as she tidied up the front check-in counter. "She was in very poor health, a diabetic possibly, for her legs were always swollen and were discolored, blue or purple. She was an invalid and lived in a wheelchair. She always was very reclusive to the point of keeping aluminum foil around her wheelchair on three sides to protect her from microwaves. She was also afraid that the Russians were going to find her and kill her."

"She also didn't like sunlight and always kept the drapes closed tightly with the shades down," added the housekeeper. "That's why guests who stay on the second floor now act so surprised to find their window drapes closed when they know that they were left open."

Steven, a professionally dressed younger man employed by the hotel, joined our conversation. "She wasn't alive when I was hired but I always heard that she loved fast food; White Castle hamburgers were her favorite to eat. All of her food was fast food from area chain restaurants, and her bodyguards would deliver her meals."

"The few times that she ever left the hotel was to visit doctors. She'd call down here and ask for the service elevator, since she'd rarely ever use the main lobby. She wanted to be avoided and left alone as much as possible. So, we'd see that the service elevator was available and send it up to her. She'd have a driver waiting near the back of the hotel to take her away and then she'd slip back inside the hotel," Liz told me.

"She never wanted me to clean any of her rooms she rented," chimed in the housekeeper. "The few times that I was with her, she was always nice to me. Miss Marys was a petite woman with graying hair and I never saw her out of the wheelchair. She was self-sufficient in the hotel room. I never changed her bed, which she didn't sleep in anyway, and I never dropped off clean towels. Her rooms were never cleaned and the fast food containers just piled up higher and higher. I think that explains why some of the guests complain about the smell of hamburgers and pizza in the rooms. It's just Miss Marys. She's not left the third floor."

"We received word on January 7, 1985, that Miss Marys had died in her room," said Liz. "She was just found dead one morning by one of her guards. No heroic efforts to save her life, no EMS. A call came down to the front desk that Miss Marys was dead and that the undertaker had been notified," added Liz.

The housekeeper nodded her head in agreement. "It was a sad day when Miss Marys died. Even though not many people knew that she existed in the hotel or had much contact with her, she impacted all of our lives." While gathering up her cleaning supplies, she turned and said, "And the scary thing is, she is still impacting our lives to this day."

9. LOVE LETTERS FROM A GHOST

Jefferson Community College
109 East Broadway

Not all ghosts are scary or harmful, and not all float through the halls of a building hoping to get delight from seeing people flee frantically from a room. On the campus of Jefferson Community College on Broadway, one such ghost does exist that apparently means no harm. Some students even refer to her affectionately as the "school spirit". The specter is believed to be Lucy Stites Barret whose husband, James Rankin Barret, built the building in his wife's memory.

Originally, the building was the Louisville Presbyterian Theological Seminary. Standing since 1903, the building was constructed of brick with a good limestone interior. It was fashioned as a Gothic masterpiece with towers, turrets, gargoyles, and great stain-glass windows. Under one roof, it housed dormitories, common areas, a chapel, and an auditorium.

In the center of the building on the second floor, a clock tower rises toward the heavens. This center section, with the arched stained glass emerald windows, is the library. This room has crisscrossing beams to support the tall ceiling. Unlit chandeliers hang down from the dark paneled ceiling to create a medieval feel for the room. Many believe that the ghost of Lucy Stites Barret haunts this chamber.

In 1968, the Jefferson Building was remodeled and became Jefferson Community College. Perhaps Lucy didn't mind the change and decided to stay on. However, it wasn't until the mid-1970s that strange incidents began to draw attention.

The ghost became so active that the Chief of Security began to keep a file to document all of the happenings his officers reported. People heard footsteps when nobody was there; the elevator went up and down on its own, carrying no visible passengers; lights flickered and dimmed when storms and power surges couldn't be blamed; flashlights with new batteries wouldn't work; doorknobs turned by an unseen hand; and mysterious letters signed with Lucy's initials (LSB) began to appear in various places. The last letter appeared in late October 1997 and said, "I am still with you."

Some attributed the letters to pranks played by students, but some of the letters revealed things that the students wouldn't know, something said or done by a person who was all alone.

Eventually, the presence took form. One security officer reported seeing a white-clothed figure standing on top of the tower and others saw a figure in the halls. Two cleaning ladies were so scared by the spooky presence that they quit their jobs and never came back.

There is an inscription over the fireplace in the library that reads:

'James Rankin Barret, in loving memory of his wife Lucy Stites Barret,
erected this building.'

Is Lucy still earthbound by this loving tribute? Does she return because of the love she knew here? Would it be possible to glimpse this ghostly figure for myself?

The fireplace that bears the inscription in memory of Lucy Stites Barret — who just may be the resident ghost!

I contacted the college and was given permission to visit. On the particular autumn day that I chose to go, the campus was almost deserted. I was met by an employee of the campus security department just inside the heavy exterior doors to the lobby. The young man was wearing a navy blue security uniform and had dozens of dangling keys suspended from his belt loop. A walkie-talkie radio, that was shoved into his back pocket, squawked nonstop. He unlocked the bolted door and the two of us began ascending an almost secret staircase to the library.

Dark wainscoting lined the

walls of this hidden passage. The boards of the steps slanted to one side due to the shifting of the aging building. Our physical weight and the guard's heavy, black military boots caused the boards to creak and groan as we made our way up the narrow passageway to the library. Standing in the mosaic-tiled hallway, he reached for a key and unlocked the door.

"Lucy Stites Barret haunts this very room," he said, in a matter of fact voice. "This was the library when the seminary occupied the campus."

He and I stood there, soaking in the surroundings. The afternoon sun was streaming through the stain-glass windows and long shadows were cast on the worn and tattered carpeting. From the high pitched ceiling, dusty chandeliers hung down by big black chains. Empty bookcases flanked both sides of the fireplace. If ever a room looked haunted, it was surely this one!

We both were drawn to the massive fireplace. I removed my hands from my pockets and rubbed my right hand over the mantle of the fireplace. It was cold to the touch and layered with dust and other tiny particles. I brushed away dead bugs and grime and, eventually, wiped my hands on the legs of my khaki trousers.

"Lucy likes this fireplace for some reason," the guard told me.

I knew why. The inscription drew my eyes and I read it aloud.

I stepped a little closer and, with the toe of my Timberland boot, I gingerly kicked one soot-covered log. Several logs tumbled forward and a puff of ash billowed out onto the hearth. The guard and I jumped back and stood facing each other.

"Do you ever experience any ghostly happenings here?" I asked.

He walked over and placed his hands on the mantle before he looked at me and spoke.

"On three separate occasions, I have answered calls on the second floor of the building and walked into this room. On this mantle, I've found notes left behind. A woman writes the notes on fine quality parchment paper in a nice script. The message is always the same: I am still with you. And the notes are simply signed with three initials: LSB. Whenever the security alarm sounds up here, I know that something I can't explain has happened."

"Do you think that somebody could be playing a prank?" I asked.

"No," he replied. "I never find anything out of order. The room is dark and no lights are turned on. All the doors are locked. It's a real mystery to me!"

He backed away and dropped his hands into his pants pockets. He leaned against the wall, crossed his right foot over the left and rested the toe of his boot on the floor. He just stared at me, waiting for a response or insight to what he just told me.

I moved back to the fireplace and ran my fingers over the letters of the inscription, tracing each one on the cold gray stone. I didn't think Lucy would mind my doing so.

By now, the guard had his keys in his hand and I felt that my work was complete. I grabbed my jacket and put it on, covering up my brown plaid shirt that I was wearing. I could still feel the cold of the stone.

We exited the once grand library and stood in the hallway. The guard turned from me and locked the door. Then he pushed his body up against it to make sure that it was secure.

We started walking down the cramped corridor of the second floor toward the secret staircase that brought us up. A clunk behind us brought us to a halt. We looked around, but we could see nothing.

"Lucy has startled many people before," he said with a smile, "or we like to think it is Lucy who roams the hallways of this building."

Another clunk sounded behind us.

"Some of the new custodial workers who work at night have complained about hearing footsteps behind them," the guard continued. "They turn around expecting to see a student or a coworker but nobody is there."

I looked over my shoulder and, again, I saw nothing. However, I could still feel the chill from the stone. Somehow, I thought he knew that and was toying with me now. On the other hand, maybe I was just experiencing something strange.

"Some tell of feeling a chilly draft of air, or a coldness that lingers," he told me. "A couple have reported seeing doors open and close by themselves. I just try to reassure them that it's Lucy and she won't hurt them at all. She's been here a long time and probably has no plans of leaving anytime soon."

However, my plans did include an immediate departure so I thanked the young man for his time and the tour. As I drove away, the cold vanished. I hadn't actually seen Lucy but I think that maybe she was there behind an invisible curtain of time, watching us and wondering why we were intruding in her favorite place.

10. SCHOOL SPIRIT

Jefferson County Traditional Middle School
1418 Morton Avenue

When people think of a traditional middle school, they tend to envision a place filled with teachers and students dedicated to teaching and learning, rules and order, and normal school spirit. Jefferson County Traditional Middle School goes one step beyond the expected. In addition to school spirit in the hearts of its students, faculty, and administration, it has the spirit of a dedicated, but deceased, principal still walking the halls and checking on operations just like she used to.

Though the school has undergone many changes over the years, it has nothing sinister in its past to lure a ghostly figure back from the grave. In fact, its history is quite normal.

The school was built in 1922 in the neighborhood just a little east of downtown Louisville. The building was dedicated as Atherton High School. This period of time was before coed schools existed. Atherton was an all-female high school with a Jewish student body.

The first principal hired was a woman by the name of Emma Woerner. She served faithfully from 1922 until her retirement thirty years later in 1953. The thirty-year period of service was evidently not enough for Miss Woerner. It is her ghost that still returns to the building where she was once in charge.

A portrait of Miss Woerner is displayed in the lobby of the school. Her likeness is fitting of an older woman with stylish graying hair and trim wire-rimmed glasses. She is seated in a chair and outfitted with a blue dress with detailed maroon collar.

Though the portrait has remained the same, time did bring about some changes. People and populations moved and communities expanded. Atherton High School moved to a different building on its present campus and the school

was renamed as Woerner Junior High School in honor of its first principal. Maybe Miss Emma Woerner appreciated the honor of having the school named after her and took it as an invitation to stay on permanently.

Today, the school is known as Jefferson County Traditional Middle School. Several principals have come and gone over the years, and each left behind their wisdom and leadership in many projects and daily pursuits. They have supported and inspired countless number of students who have climbed those marble steps from the main entrance and traveled the corridors of the building. No one, however, surpassed Miss Woerner in bringing spirit to the school.

Miss Woerner has made her presence known on several occasions. Those who have had contact, or face-to-face encounters, are all credible witnesses. Some of the school custodians were willing to share their experiences with me.

A custodian named Larry recalled, "One night, I was working on the third floor in the older part of the building. I'd just begun sweeping the hallway and I was near the corner where the two halls intersect. At that, the only footsteps I heard were my own against the polished floor. But as I moved around with my broom, I began to hear another set of footsteps."

"Did they continue very long?" I asked.

"Yes," he said. "I kept hearing them while I worked. I knew nobody else was supposed to be on that floor."

"What did they sound like?" I asked him. "Were they light or heavy?"

"It sounded to me like they were a woman's shoes," he responded thoughtfully. "I heard the heels click clearly against the hardwood. It wasn't at all like the sneakers I was wearing. It sounded so real that I stopped to see who was coming. I leaned my broom against the lockers and waited.

"The sound of the footsteps was getting louder. I knew whoever it was would be rounding the corner any second and we'd meet face-to-face.

"I couldn't figure out why anyone would be walking down the hall at that hour since the school was closed, but I stood prepared to call out a greeting. And then I saw her! My mouth opened, but my words froze in my throat. She passed right in front of me, wearing that blue colored suit! I knew who it was because I'd seen that portrait."

"Did she look like a real person?" I asked.

"Not really," he said, shaking his head. "She was almost transparent. Yet I could tell who she was. There was no doubt in my mind. It was Miss Woerner. I felt a draft of cold air pass in front of me as she went by. The air around me was still normal so I took the broom and went back to work."

Pam, a custodian with long, dark hair, told me what happened to her.

"I'll tell you when it started," she said. "When I first started working here, Miss Woerner's portrait was hanging in the back of the stage, almost like it was in storage or something. I don't think that she liked that very much."

"I wonder why," I said.

"Maybe it made her feel unappreciated!" said Pam. "I just know that there was something about cleaning that stage area I never liked. When I'd be there gathering trash, setting up chairs, or just running the dust mop, I would feel like her eyes were following me."

"Do you think that she was there?" I asked.

"I'm sure that it was just my imagination," she laughed. "Yet it gave me the creeps to be there. I was glad when somebody in the administrative office decided to move her portrait back to the main hallway where everybody could see it."

"Do you get the creepy feeling in the stage area now?" I asked her.

"No," she answered, "but now I feel like she is watching me in the front hall. I won't look at that portrait."

"She can certainly make her presence known without actually appearing," said another custodian, who stopped stocking his cart to tell his story. "Now, this happened to me and I still cannot explain it. I was on the third floor one night in the old part of the building.

"I had just finished one room, so I turned out the light and started down the hallway. I don't know what made me do it, but I turned and looked back down the hall. I noticed that the light in that classroom was on yet I remembered distinctly that I had turned it off. I walked back down there and peeped through that small panel of glass. I thought that somebody was in there, but I didn't see anyone.

"I unlocked the door and reached inside and turned the light out again. It puzzled me that the light had come back on. I locked the door and started down the hall again. This time, I couldn't resist taking one more look. When I turned around, I saw that the lights were back on again.

"I stood there and looked at one end of the hall and then the other. Nothing moved but there was a sound. I decided just to leave those lights on!"

Bill Neace serves as the head custodian at the school now. He joined the staff in 1996 and worked here until 2001. He recently returned to work at Jefferson County Traditional Middle School.

During his early tenure at the school, it wasn't long before he became acquainted with Miss Woerner.

"I was cleaning the auditorium seats when I started hearing the sound of a child crying," he told me. "I stopped, walked around, moved backstage, and even opened the fire escape doors to find the child. I looked all around but there was nobody there.

"I radioed downstairs to the other janitor and told him about the crying sound. He claimed that he heard a child crying down on his floor but he couldn't locate the source.

"The crying child didn't disturb me as much as seeing Miss Woerner upstairs. It was late in the fall season so it was dark outdoors. I had most of the hallway lights on so I could see clearly. For some reason, I glanced down the hall and saw an elderly woman coming up the stairwell. I stopped and thought: who is that old woman coming up the stairs?

"I had the doors propped open and she came right up on the landing. I started walking toward her to see who she was and where she was going. Now, I am a big guy and she couldn't miss me at all but she never looked my way.

"I followed her and she walked into the gymnasium. Those doors were closed and I knew that, once inside the gym, I would have her trapped. She couldn't leave unless she exited out a narrow fire escape. Since the gym is on the third floor of the building, it wasn't likely that an elderly woman would go down the fire escape."

"No," I agreed. "That would not be likely."

"Well, once inside the gym, I looked to the left and to the right and saw only a basketball on the floor. The intruder was not to be found in there. The only other place she could be hiding was the locker room. My thoughts were racing.

"Could she be here? What is with this woman?

"I made my way toward the locker room doors and listened. I put my hand on the brass handle and opened the door just a crack.

"'Is anyone in here?' I called out.

"I heard no answer so I repeated the question. Still, no response was given.

"I opened the door wider and stepped inside of the locker room. It was deadly silent. The sound of my sneakers squeaking on the sticky floor echoed eerily. I made my way along the wall of lockers and passed the stalls of toilets. The entire time, I kept my eyes focused on the only exit. I heard no footsteps but I could hear the occasional sound of water dripping into a sink. I walked the entire locker room and found no trace of the mysterious woman.

"I left the locker room and headed toward the fire escape door. I opened it and stepped out to the black metal landing. I looked down the three flights of stairs and toward the back of the building. At the end is a seven-foot tall fence and gate that leads to an alley. I doubt seriously that she could have escaped down those steps and climbed that fence.

"I stepped back inside the gym, pulled the fire escape door closed, and secured it. It remains a mystery to me to this day. I know that the woman I saw bore a strong resemblance to the portrait that hangs downstairs. Maybe Miss Woerner had heard a child crying like I did and was on her way to give comfort and assistance."

I currently teach in the haunted school building and I think that perhaps I have had a brush with the supernatural. One day, I invited a good friend, Roberta Simpson Brown, who is an author and paranormal investigator, to speak to my reading classes. During a break, the two of us were walking in the third floor corridor. Mrs. Brown had brought along two instruments for measuring paranormal activity-a set of dowsing rods (a simple tool used to determine the presence of ghosts) and an EMF meter (an instrument that measures electro-magnetic fields).

Mrs. Brown was holding the dowsing rods as we passed the library.

"Is there a ghost here?" I asked.

The rods immediately swung wide open, which indicates a "yes". Mrs. Brown and I just stood there looking at each other, and then down at the dowsing rods in their open position.

Then we began to hear a loud beeping sound. Again, we stood there looking at each other.

"What's that noise?" I asked her.

"My EMF meter!" she answered.

Reaching into her purse, Mrs. Brown pulled out the EMF meter and looked at it.

"Look!" she said. "The needle is all the way over in the red as far as it can go!"

I looked and confirmed that she was right.

"This is really weird!" she exclaimed. "I did not have the meter turned on when I put it in my purse! The power came on all by itself!"

"Are the batteries old?" I asked. "Maybe they are acting up."

"I put new batteries in this morning," she insisted. "Something turned the power on!"

The meter continued to beep and the needle stayed in the high intensity zone. We decided to walk to different locations and see what happened. At every other spot we chose, the dowsing rods did not open and the meter remained quiet. The needle dropped back to normal. When we returned to the hallway outside of the library, we again got reactions from the dowsing rods and the EMF meter. Apparently, something hovering near the library wanted to make its presence known to us.

Is the ghost of Miss Woerner really haunting the school on Morton Avenue? You might want to come by and see for yourself. If a stern looking, gray-haired woman meets you at the door, just smile and wish her "happy ghoul" days!

11. THE HAUNTED SUIT OF ARMOR

Joe Ley's Antiques
615 East Market Street

Joe Ley's Antiques is listed in many travel brochures as one of Louisville's top lures to tourists and residents alike. Indeed, it is difficult to resist the mystique and marvels of this vintage delight. Located in downtown at 615 East Market Street in the historic Hiram Roberts School, which was built in 1890, Joe Ley's houses more than two acres of fine antique and bargain-hunters' treasures on three floors.

This antique emporium/museum has a one-time admission of one dollar and is a repository of the households and businesses of bygone days. This place has a little bit of everything from architectural objects to antique glassware, furniture, farm implements, toys, tools, old 78 records, roadside signs, kitchen equipment, ornaments, and, as one librarian put it, a collection of rather disturbing circus props. Some people feel that the old building has several eerie aspects and maybe a ghost or two.

Extreme rumors have it that Joe Ley's is a creepy feeling place and that the walls in the basement sometimes bleed. Another rumor that has been circulating around Louisville for years is that a suit of armor is haunted and actually moves around. Owners have never confirmed these rumors but I wanted to find out more for myself.

My investigation showed that nobody in the store has any record on the history of the suit of armor such as its age, where it came from, or any testimony from the previous owner. It's one of those pieces that has been in the store for a long time and still attracts a lot of attention.

Employees are generally reluctant to discuss the haunted aspect of the store but, during my visit to investigate, I encountered a sales associate who agreed to talk to me about the armor if I withheld his identity. I can say that he was a brown-haired young man sporting a beard and wearing shorts and a polo shirt.

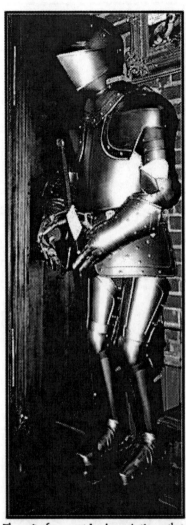

The suit of armor at Joe Leys Antiques that allegedly moves around by itself

He led me into the first room of the first floor and allowed me to take several pictures.

"This is the suit of armor that is restless," he told me. "For some reason, it moves about during the night."

I moved around, examining the posture of the suit of armor as he continued to speak.

"For the last couple of years," he said, "the first employee who opens up for the day comes into this room to document the position of the suit of armor. It's been found with the arms raised or slightly bent at the elbows. Also, the knees have been bent and one leg has been seen in a forward position."

"Just like it was walking," I commented.

"Yes," he agreed.

"Has anything else happened?" I inquired.

"Yes," he answered. "I think that this is the strangest of all. For a while, we would place this heavy table in front of the suit of armor. And you know what?"

"What?" I asked.

"The next morning," he confided, "the table would be shoved aside as if the table was blocking its passage and it just reached down and moved it out of the way."

"That is strange," I agreed. "Are you sure somebody wasn't just playing a trick to scare you?"

"Whatever it is that is inhabiting the armor hasn't scared anybody who works here," he assured me. "We have cameras for security and we ruled out any prank pretty quickly."

"Does it move at any other time that you know of?" I asked.

"No," he said. "We don't know of anytime during the business day that it has moved on its own. As you can tell, it is too heavy to be moved by a customer."

Whether he was telling me the truth or making up a story just to entertain me, it certainly had the effect of sending shivers up and down my spine. His story did confirm the rumor that I had heard and I had no reason not to believe the young man.

As I advise all of my readers and guests on the ghost walks, it is always a good thing to investigate for yourself and make up your own mind.

So the next time that you are traveling along the East Market corridor of downtown Louisville, it might pay to drop by Joe Ley's Antiques. Besides being a great antique store, it has proved to be a popular place for the filming of music videos, movies, and commercials. You can view it as a museum of Louisville's history or you can browse and shop for a bargain. You might even be able to "scare up" a ghost from that old armor that will "suit" your fancy!

12. GHOSTS OF THE PALACE THEATER

The Louisville Palace Theater
625 South Fourth Street

The Palace Theater is one of Louisville's grandest movie venues. Designed by John Eberson, the theater is said to have cost an estimated 1.2 million dollars to build. The luxury of the Palace has drawn and enchanted patrons and workers both in life and death.

From the history of this magnificent structure come both legends and factual information to support the theory that the Palace Theater is a uniquely haunted place!

The doors swung open on September 1, 1928, as Loew's and United Artist State Theater. In 1954, it was bought and renamed the United Artists. In 1963, the balcony was blocked off and a wall was built that accommodated a large screen, which created a second theater housed under one roof. It opened as the Penthouse Theater.

During the decline of the downtown business and retail district, the doors were finally closed on the theater complex, silencing the movie venue for many years. Darkness fell on the once grand lobby that showcased the 130 busts that stare down from the vaulted ceiling. The statues in the theater that created a Spanish Baroque garden became black silhouettes from another time period covered in cobwebs.

But during the restoration in the 1980s, the balcony wall and screen were removed. And the theater was renamed the Palace Theater. During this labor of love, it was restored to its original design, complete with a garden scene, statues, trees, soaring birds, twinkling stars, and clouds for a nighttime sky.

All you have to do is simply look up to see historic figures and famous faces. But as you are looking up, you might wonder if someone or something is looking down at you!

It was during the restoration and reopening that workers began reporting strange sounds, sightings, and maintenance problems. During these years of restoration, the construction workers, electricians, and painters all labored for many months inside the Palace and had experiences with something, whether you want to call it a ghost or not. They were not alone while working there and it didn't take them long to realize it!

The stories I heard about the Palace were intriguing to me and made me want to find out all I could about the theater as a haunted site.

One worker told of seeing an older man in work clothes sitting in the balcony looking down at him. Another worker, who had fallen asleep while painting the ceiling from some scaffolding, swore that a ghostly voice woke him just as he was about to roll off of the scaffold and plunge to his death. Others vowed that they heard whistling, unseen footsteps, and doors opening and closing. Tools would be moved to an area where the men had not been working. They also claim to have found the name Ferdinand scribbled in the dust in the basement. They believed that the name referred to the chief engineer of the Loews United Artists Theater, a man named Ferdinand Frisch, who died of a massive heart attack in the basement office on October 27, 1965.

These stories were so fascinating to me that I began my own search for eyewitness accounts. I was able to talk to several employees who had their own stories worth telling and adding to my collection.

My first interview was with an office worker named Alision.

"The office is next to the building, so we have to go outside and enter the theater through the front doors," she explained. "Just inside the foyer is a grand staircase that leads to the mezzanine level. On more than one occasion, I have been stopped in my tracks by seeing a woman dressed in what looks like clothing from the 1940s standing on the stairs. Her back is to me as if she is ascending the steps. I've called out to her to ask if I could help her, since the building is locked. She'll turn slightly and I can see that she is wearing white gloves, heels, and a brownish, tan tweed suit and a hat. The startling thing about her appearance is that she has no face! Her other bodily features are present but she just has no face! That can't be explained as far as I am concerned."

"Does she ever try to communicate with you in any way?" I asked.

"No," said Alision. "I guess that she will always remain a nameless movie-goer, stuck in a bygone time."

The next employee that I interviewed one night was a tall man with blond hair who preferred to remain nameless.

"My plumbing company has the service contract on the Palace to repair and service the plumbing throughout the building, restrooms, water fountains, as well as backstage in the dressing rooms or showers," he said. "I recall being down in the sub-basement one time. I was working alone or, at least, I thought I was alone. But something kept following me. I could hear footsteps behind me but every time that I'd stop and look over my shoulder to see who had come down, there would be no one there!

"Something else weird always happened when I was working. I'd lay a wrench down, or a tape measure, anything, and turn my back. When I'd reach for it, it would be gone. I'd usually find it some place else where I hadn't been working at all.

"Some of the carpenters and electricians had similar experiences when they were working. We'd end up outside in the alley exchanging stories about the ghosts in there. Some of the guys talked about seeing two ghosts. Sometimes in the balcony, other times on the stage. Those guys seemed to think that the ghosts were male because of their size. One guy was pretty close to one and he claimed that it had a grayish cast to it. But I've never seen one. Don't want to, either!"

One of the theater's historians contributed a story about the palace that is one of my favorites.

"The Palace has one unique feature in the women's restroom," he informed me. "One stall that has an adult-size commode also has a tiny, child-size commode. It's really a rare piece of plumbing and functional for the time when mothers had small children that needed to use the facilities.

"What has been strange to me is that when I'd be walking along the mezzanine level and approach the women's restroom, I'd hear giggling. Sometimes I'd hear the sound of running shoes on the tile floor. I'd go investigate and, as I got closer to the entrance, the stall door would suddenly slam! I'd rush in, thinking that I'd caught an adolescent prankster, but my search would be fruitless. I've seen little feet and little tiny legs in that one particular stall in the far corner, but my investigations all come up empty.

"Oh, I tried to reason it out by reassuring myself that some other employee had brought his or her daughter to work and that was who I was hearing in the building. But I know that there is no reason or logic to it. Whatever footsteps and giggling sound I hear are definitely not from anyone in this world."

Perhaps the most enduring and endearing Palace ghost story is that of Barney, a projectionist employed by Loew's during the 1930s. He was very dedicated and enjoyed his position very much. He would always stay at his post even when the temperature in the projection booth got very high.

Then, one day in the middle of a movie showing, Barney became ill and suffered a heart attack. His coworkers rushed to his aid and did what they could to prolong his life. Since the projection booth was in a higher area, it was difficult to rush Barney out of the theater and to the hospital.

Thinking quickly, employees removed a door from its hinges and used it as a stretcher. Barney was laid on the door and his coworkers carried him as carefully as they could down the stairs toward the closest exit. They knew that Barney needed immediate attention to survive the heart attack but, in the end, it was not the attack that took his life.

In the midst of the excitement and panic, the coworkers neglected to secure Barney to the door. As they descended the steep steps, the door slipped and got away from the men. It fell on the stairs and then Barney fell hard onto the door. The impact broke Barney's back and he died instantly. It's no wonder that it's been reported that Barney's ghost haunts the Palace Theater!

I spoke with a dark-haired worker in his late thirties who believes that he saw Barney once.

"I've worked as a lighting technician here for many years," he told me. "My company has the contract here as well as a couple of other theaters around town.

"The show was having a rehearsal one night and I was manning some spotlights for the upcoming show. I knew that I was alone in the booth but I felt strange eyes staring at me from somewhere. The temperature suddenly dropped like nothing that I was expecting.

"I turned quickly and saw a man wearing a little narrow necktie, a while shirt, dark pants, and a hat. He was dressed as a man would have been clothed in the 1930s. I just stared at the guy until I realized that I could see right through him! I blinked and he was gone. Then I knew that I had seen a ghost."

On more than one occasion, spotlights have been moved and projection cameras relocated as if a movie was going to be shown soon. Folks just blame it on Barney.

Another worker, a young woman with long blond hair, feels that she had a personal encounter with Barney even though she didn't actually see him.

"It was during a concert, a Christian concert as a matter of fact," she said. "I had my hair pulled back in a ponytail and had my spotlight on a performer. With most spotlights, a beam of light is reflected from the backside of the spotlight. From the corner of my eye, I saw something or someone break that beam of light that was cast on the back wall. I turned to see who it was but nobody was there. Then I felt someone pull my ponytail!

"We'd been joking about the ghost of Barney so I thought that one of the guys was playing a prank on me, just trying to spook me. I turned and looked but, again, nobody was there! Someone kept pulling my hair, not once, but several times! I'll admit that I was a little spooked by now. Nobody was near me when my hair was being pulled. Sure, I'd heard stories about Barney but I'd never seen him. I was puzzled by the sensation of having my hair pulled. I was just standing and slowly rotating around, just trying to figure out who pulled my hair. With my particular spotlight, a small beam of light is projected from the rear of the light. Depending upon the distance between the machine and the nearest wall, determines the size of the light that is shown on the wall. I was simply rotating around and I was saying to myself, 'Okay Barney, if it is really and truly you, prove it to me.' Just as I finished that statement, I was facing the ray of light on the back wall. Suddenly, a dark silhouette of a man passed in front of the light casting a shadow on the wall. That made a believer out of me.

"I finally said, 'Barney, just stop it!' And it never happened again!"

"Maybe he heard you," I suggested.

"I guess he did," she agreed. "Maybe I scared him off."

Some ushers and custodians told me that they had strange experiences, too. As they approach the balcony from the side stairwells, they've seen an individual seated in the balcony watching them. They'll call out to him and ask if they can help, but there will be no audible response. His body will begin to fade away and the next sound will be that of the cushioned seat bouncing up.

One individual mentioned seeing a man in older clothing standing at the balcony railing.

"Did you call to him?" I asked.

"Yes," he replied. "I asked him what he wanted."

"Did he respond?" I asked him.

"No," he said. "He simply faded away after a few seconds."

A long time volunteer usher complains that Barney likes to play pranks sometimes.

"I close the doors to the fire escape but they keep coming open. I think Barney is the responsible party who keeps opening them."

Is Barney a creature of habit that keeps coming back to the place where he so faithfully carried out his work? Or, in Barney's memory, is he returning to the stairwell where he was dropped and met his death? Is he doomed somehow to relive that over and over throughout eternity?

Whatever the answers are, they continue to elude those of us who investigate. It is comforting to those of us who are patrons of the Palace to know that the ghosts there never harm anyone since they seem to enjoy the performances and might turn up there in the audience right beside me-or you!

13. APARTMENTS FOR APPARITIONS

The Mansarrat / Fifth Ward School Building
747 South Fifth Street

At the corner of Fifth and York Streets stands an impressive, red brick Italian Renaissance Revival building that has served as a school, a Civil War hospital, an army dormitory, museums and storage for the Louisville Free Public Library and, finally, as apartments.

As different tenants have come and gone over the years, one thing has remained constant. Along with students, soldiers, and ordinary citizens who have occupied this place at one time or another, there are ghosts! That part of the building's history never faded from view.

Chris, a TV reporter friend of mine, first made me aware of this ghostly activity. This young man, with a big smile and tousled hair, appeared to be the least likely person to have a ghost as a roommate. However, he assured me that he did!

"I've seen the ghost of a woman in my apartment," he confided to me. "With the building's background, I guess that I shouldn't be surprised."

You would be surprised, though, if you looked only at the building's exterior. It is graced with nine-foot rounded arched windows that illuminated the classrooms back in the 1800s.

The first school to occupy that corner burned in 1854. From the ashes and mortar rose the Fifth Ward School, which opened in 1857.

The usual subjects were taught at the time and an emphasis on shop courses was offered to boys to master a trade. Certainly there was nothing supernatural about any of that, but conditions were soon to change.

The building began to see many different uses over the years. A few years after the 1857 school opening, the Civil War raged in this area. The Union Army

used the building as a hospital for the wounded and dying soldiers. Maybe this planted the seeds for later paranormal growth and activity.

The city of Louisville rebounded after the Civil War and the population grew and spread south. The building was used as a school again but its name was changed to the Seventh Ward School. Then, as demographics changed, the school's doors were closed once again.

The army again realized the value of the property and restored the building for use as a dormitory for soldiers on leave from Fort Knox during World War II.

Shortly after the war was over, the Louisville Free Public Library occupied the property with various forms of museums and storage of books.

Today, the building is far from abandoned. In 1982, it was converted into 18 apartments and renamed the Monsarrat.

"When I first moved to Louisville as a television news reporter," my friend Chris told me, "I had an apartment in the Monsarret. I knew that they had remodeled the building and redesigned the rooms to make for better living space. However, I did not know that a ghostly presence did not realize that this living space was now mine and not hers."

"You actually witnessed ghostly activity in your apartment?" I asked, really interested now.

"Yes," Chris insisted. "It's true! A woman began making appearances at night. I saw her walk across my bedroom. She would pass near the foot of my bed."

"Wow!" I joked. "What was she wearing? A fancy nightgown?"

"No," he laughed. "Nothing like that. The clothing looked like a Civil War dress, with a high collar and a big, full skirt. Her entire body, her hair, her face, and the dress were all bluish gray."

"Are you sure that you weren't dreaming?" I asked.

"I thought that I might be at first," he replied, "or that my eyes were playing tricks on me, but it happened too often for me just to dismiss it as my imagination or eyesight. I actually saw her."

"Where did she come from when she would appear?" I asked him. "Did she just suddenly materialize out of thin air?"

"No," he said. "That was the strangest thing. She would pass through one wall into my room. Then she would walk across my room and disappear into my walk-in closet."

"Did you ever follow her to try and find out what she was doing in there?" I inquired.

"I did once," he told me. "One time when she paraded across the room and vanished into the closet, my curiosity got the best of me. I got out of bed and stepped to the closet door. My plan was to confront her and ask what she was doing. I tried to be brave because I needed to know once and for all what was going on."

He paused and smiled.

"Did you find out?" I prompted.

"It's funny now that I think about it," he laughed. "I'm glad that nobody saw me! I must have been a funny looking sight. I stood just outside of my closet door and listened but there was only silence. I couldn't stand the suspense any longer, so I decided that any action was better than no action at all.

"I placed both hands on the two doorknobs that opened and closed my closet doors. I didn't know what to expect to see or hear, or what I would have done if the woman were inside the closet. I just knew that I had to check it out if I wanted to get any sleep that night.

"I took a deep breath and swung the doors open wide until they banged against the walls. She was not there!

"Still not satisfied, I jumped inside and pushed aside all of my hanging clothes. I thrashed around like a wild man and found nothing out of order. Nobody was lurking in the corners or hiding behind my shirts and pants.

"Of course, my clothes were all bunched up now and my shoes were scattered on the floor where I had knocked them in my frenzy to seek out the spirit. A couple hangers clanging together made the only sound in the closet. Whoever I had seen simply wasn't there.

"Defeated, I put my closet in order and went back to bed."

"I guess you were really relieved that you didn't find her," I commented.

He shook his head.

"Not really," he said. "In a way, I was disappointed. I wanted to know who she was and why she kept returning. I'll always wonder where she came from and who or what she was looking for. Since she was dressed in Civil War clothing, perhaps she was looking for a soldier who never returned from the war."

Some people say that because of the years that the building was used as a hospital for soldiers, the ghosts of some who died there might still linger inside those walls. Their bodies were removed one by one, but maybe their spirits remained.

While in the basement, people have heard distant cries and moans but they can't find any explanation or origin for the mournful sounds. Some believe that they come from ailing or dying soldiers in another time.

Some descriptions give specific details that may offer support to this theory. Heavy footsteps have been heard, as if one soldier is dragging his foot across the wooden floor. Strange, unearthly odors can be smelled upon opening closet doors. Some say that it is the smell of death and dying.

People turn and look over their shoulders when they are downstairs but they see nothing ghostly behind them. They make up excuses and try to figure out a logical explanation for the mystery. So far, none of them have been successful in their endeavors.

If you plan to rent one of the apartments at the Monsarrat, be prepared to share your living space with a roommate whose name is not on the lease and who pays no rent! Remember, from the ghost's point of view, you may be the one whose presence cannot be explained!

14. THE HOUSE OF PAIN AND SUFFERING

The Old House on Fifth Street
432 South Fifth Street

The old green canopy with the white script that reads The Old House should perhaps be reworded to read The House of Pain and Suffering. This old, three-story townhouse at 432 South Fifth Street is vacant now, but something about the old house causes those who pass by to pause and glance at the upstairs window. Some take a second look because they think that they see a form standing by the window in that empty old place. On a recent tour, one of the ladies in the group was certain that she saw the curtain move.

Is it a shadow or a draft in the old house that causes these illusions, or is the old house haunted by someone who suffered and died there in the past? Perhaps the answer lies in the things that happened through the years inside those walls.

The house does have a rich history and many people have vivid memories of this location. It was built during 1829 and it was the first to be heated by steam and to have electricity. The house is characteristic of the type of buildings that lined 3rd, 4th, and 5th streets during the early 19th century. Throughout its history, it was used as a residence, medical and dental offices, and a restaurant.

During the 1800s, the house was used as a residence and medical office for Dr. William A. McDowell.

Dr. McDowell was born in Mercer County, Kentucky, on March 21, 1795. Soon after receiving his medical degree from Medical College in Philadelphia, he formed a partnership with his uncle, Dr. Ephraim McDowell of Danville, Kentucky.

Later, blazing a trail for research and treatment of tuberculosis, Dr. McDowell moved to Louisville and opened up a medical practice in the townhouse at 432 South Fifth Street. He utilized three of the bedrooms on the upstairs level for experimental medicine.

Dr. McDowell was known as having treatments for tuberculosis, some extreme and some quaint. One of his known practices was to send his patients to live in Mammoth Cave. The cave provided a constant temperature and fresh air away from the dirty city. Unfortunately, the cold, damp cave did not produce the results that he had hoped for. They were not cured and some were even worse than before.

Unfortunately, many patients returned to Dr. McDowell from Mammoth Cave, and he took them into his home when their frail bodies would arrive and ascend the steps leading to the front door.

Pale and sickly patients would move lifelessly throughout the house, pull back the lace curtains, and look down on the street. Finally, they would retreat to their bedrooms where they would live out their remaining days gasping for breath under Dr. McDowell's care.

Is it the ghost of one of these patients that is the shadowy form by the window? Is it the invisible hand of one of these poor people that moves the curtain back?

There are tales of a ghost that lingers there that may not be one of the patients. Reports have been made of a tall male figure moving about the third floor. Could it be the spirit of Dr. McDowell? His features were of a handsome man, tall and strong, with blond colored hair and blue eyes. In fact, he stood at a height of 6'2". He would fit the description of the male specter seen on the third floor of the house. The sound of heavy footsteps heard traveling from room to room could easily have been his.

Dr. McDowell died of a diseased heart on December 10, 1853. He was living in the state of Indiana at that time, but his body was transported back to Louisville and interred at Cave Hill Cemetery.

Perhaps his heart was always in Louisville where he worked so hard to care for his patients. Those who believe that they have seen his ghost, as it would enter a darkened bedroom, have expressed no fear from his presence. They claim that he would enter a bedchamber and move closer to the bedside. His sunken eyes would stare down at the person lying in bed. Those who have encountered him state that it is more of a kind, calming presence, intending to bring comfort and not fear.

Could the shadowy figure at the window be the good doctor himself? Is he lurking in the shadows to see if the Angel of Death is coming for another victim? Nobody can offer the answer to this puzzle. We can only make predictions. Maybe Dr. McDowell still roams the house, trying to bring comfort to those who may remain inside the brick walls of the old house.

Perhaps these hauntings could come from another source. If you are one of those people who dread going to the dentist, you might believe that the dental practices there were the source of enough pain and suffering to make the site memorable to those who came for treatment and passed on long ago.

For thirty years, the home was the property of two dentists-Drs. J. F. Canine (who lived there with his wife Elizabeth) and J. A. McClelland, the later of whom purchased the house in 1868.

Canine installed steam-powered drills and electric lights, while McClelland worked extensively with the use of celluloid in dentures.

In this rebuilding period shortly after the Civil War, dentistry was still a new form of health care for teeth. It was only a luxury for the wealthy. Still, dentistry came with its own form of pain and suffering. Abscessed and injured teeth were removed, and surgeries were performed on patients seeking relief from dental problems.

Maybe one of those suffering dental patients stands eternally by the window, hoping to see a way to escape the steam-powered drill!

Some have less painful memories of The Old House from the time that it was a restaurant. Since teeth played an important role when visiting the restaurant, some patrons thought that it was amusingly ironic that dental offices had been there before.

A woman named Erma Dick operated this Louisville premiere restaurant for fine French cuisine. She appropriately called her restaurant The Old House. Between the years 1946 until the mid 1980s, the house was a centerpiece for downtown dining. Erma entertained a variety of customers including Walt Disney, cowboy-singer Tex Ritter, actors Raymond Burr and Caesar Romero, and former presidents Gerald Ford and Ronald Reagan.

The doctors, dentists, patients, and local and celebrity patrons no longer come through the front door for treatments or food. But something is inside there, quietly watching the living pass by. What is it waiting for? What does it want?

15. ETERNAL INCARCERATION

Old City Jail
514 West Liberty

Louisville has many things for which it has received recognition: the Kentucky Derby, the Louisville Slugger, the *Belle of Louisville*, Actor's Theater, Thunder Over Louisville (the largest fireworks display and air show in North America), the Louisville Zoo, the J. B. Speed Art Museum, etc. It also has a large number of fine hotels and many hospitals, which have pioneered many state-of-the-art procedures in the field of medicine. It also has the Old Jefferson County Jail, which received a kind of recognition that the city of Louisville would probably like to forget.

The Old City Jail had one distinct honor. It took second place to the Cook County Jail in Chicago, Illinois, as being the worst jail in the nation. Because of the things that occurred there, the old facility is said to be haunted!

In 1902, construction on the impressive red stone building was started at the corner of Liberty and 6th Street. The building was completed in 1905, with 240 operating cells. It was designed by the architecture firm of DX Murphy and Company, the same company that designed the infamously haunted Waverly Hills Sanatorium (the old tuberculosis hospital off Dixie Highway) and the old Manual High School. You can see similarities in all three of these buildings. The old jail is listed on the National Register of Historic Places because of its architectural significance.

It is an intriguing piece of property. It has two unique architectural designs that share one roof. The eastern side housed the administration, cafeteria, and hospital. The western side, complete with four floors, accommodated the incarcerated population for periods of less than one year.

The building was designed with three floors for men and one floor for

women. The large, freestanding cellblock was located on the 6th Street side. The other side, which housed the women, was U-shaped.

From the exterior, the building resembles a massive castle which was meant to create the illusion of being a fortress. The massive structure was also meant to discourage inmates' associates, who were still walking the streets, from attempting to assist an inmate with an escape. This did not seem to work very well, however. In spite of the efforts of officials to thwart any attempts to get out, escapes were numerous.

The old jail had two unique features that thrust it into the spotlight. A new state-of-the-art cell locking system on each tier made it possible for the guards to open one cell door or multiple cell doors. Another feature was an underground tunnel used to transfer prisoners from the jail to the courthouse for their arraignments, hearings, etc., without taking them up to street level. Apparently, the tunnels were supposed to lessen the chances of prisoners escaping and to increase the safety of the general public who might be on the street at the times when prisoners had to be moved. They also provided a place for abuse to go unseen.

Due to overcrowding and deteriorating conditions, the building closed in the 1970s when a new correctional facility and Hall of Justice opened in Louisville.

For several years, the old jail sat abandoned and in a state of limbo. Finally, enough visionaries banded together to save the building from the wrecking ball. They thought that the magnificent old structure could be put to better use.

The building was completely gutted and remodeled to become an office building for Jefferson County. Now, instead of officially housing prisoners, it houses the Jefferson County Public Law Library; storage areas for archives and records of Jefferson County; conference rooms; and offices for elected officials.

Stories circulate, however, indicating that even death did not provide some prisoners with an escape. The torture, neglect, and abuse that evidently occurred to cause this jail to earn such a bad reputation may be holding these poor souls behind invisible bars throughout eternity. A door in time slammed, locking the spirits of the dead in the same building as the living.

During my personal investigation of the old jail, I found very few traces of the building's history or the actual treatment of prisoners. Local historians had little information about the old jail. There was no official confirmation of ghosts on record. Two ladies working in Property Management confirmed that the jail was the second worst in the nation and that the tunnel does exist. I also talked to some workers who passed on personal experiences and rumors that they had heard.

It is said that some policemen refuse to be alone in the basement because it is so unnerving. It is also said that, even standing on the street, you can sometimes hear the iron jail doors clanking and the moans of long dead prisoners rising up through the street grates.

Security workers have had several eerie incidents occur while on duty.

"I think this is something pretty funny," one worked grinned. "I think ghosts and plumbing go together. They must be attracted to water."

"What makes you think that?" I asked.

"The toilets flush all by themselves," he explained. "When our shift begins, we walk the interior of the building and make sure that everything like water and lights are turned off. On another trip, we'll hear the water running somewhere and we'll assume someone left a water faucet turned on and we missed it on our first walkthrough. We know that no one else is in the building."

"That must be a spooky feeling," I commented.

"Yes," he agreed. "It makes you feel creepy when you can't explain something. I really believe that something is haunting the restrooms in this building."

An older African American man who worked there nodded in agreement.

"I've worked security here for a number of years," he said. "The security system is pretty sensitive. Red lights will go off on the main computer system if someone is on the upper floors."

"Does that happen often?" I asked.

"Fairly often," he told me. "We know that we are the only ones in the building but we go investigate anyway. We keep in radio communication with each other, thinking that we might be getting ready to nab a trespasser. We reach the area, call out for the trespasser to come out of hiding, and wait. We stand there with our flashlights on, but nothing happens. We flip on the main lighting system only to find that nobody is present."

"Does it happen every night?" I questioned.

"No, not every night," he said, "but it's happened too many times to be dismissed as a fluke or computer malfunction."

"What do you think is going on?" I asked him.

"I don't know," he answered thoughtfully. "I just know that something is opening doors which triggers the silent alarm down here. Even the surveillance camera picks up some shadowy form moving down the hallways but when we get there, it's vanished."

Security workers are not the only ones to experience strange things. A judge working late in his office is said to have heard groans and moans coming from the long-gone cell area. He investigated and found himself alone! He had no explanation for what he had heard, but he was certain that he had heard something!

A man who prefers to remain anonymous gave me a similar account.

"I was working in my office one evening," he told me, "when something kept disturbing my work. I could hear footsteps on the tiled hallway floor.

"At first I thought little of it. Even though the floor I was on was supposed to be deserted at that hour, I knew that a few security guards and maybe some custodians were still present on other floors.

"After hearing the footsteps a couple more times, I stepped to the office door and looked up and down the hallway. It was dimly lit and the light cast shadows of eerie lines and shapes on the walls. However, I saw nobody so I went back to my desk.

"Then, again in the distance, I heard footsteps start up. Now it sounded as if more than one person was walking. I ruled out custodial workers. These footsteps had the heavy thud of boots.

"Of course, knowing that this was an old jail, I let my mind race and imagined some guards wearing their boots while leading the prisoners to their cells. I tried to shake my head and blame the noise on real live workers, but that just didn't settle with me."

"Did you continue to hear these footsteps?" I asked.

"Yes," he said, "but the noises intensified as the time passed."

"Do you mean the footsteps?" I inquired.

"Yes," he answered, "but there were other noises now. Cries and moans echoed through the building!"

"Did you go investigate?" I asked.

"Oh, yes," he continued. "I went out of the office and walked down the hallway, but the sounds that I was hearing seemed to be moving further away from me. It was like some unseen visitor was moving ahead of me."

"Where did the sounds go?" I asked him.

"That was the troubling thing!" he exclaimed. "When I got to the end of the hallway, the sounds all stopped! The silence made my skin tingle. Then, all of a sudden, they started again, only this time they were coming from behind me in the corridor I had just walked down. Whatever I had been following was now following me! The footsteps and the low moans were advancing my way and I had no idea of how they could possibly have gotten by me to get behind! I realized that I was trapped in a dead end hallway!"

"Good heavens!" I gasped. "What did you do?"

"It really got to me," he admitted. "My heart was racing and my hands were cold. What on earth was coming that I couldn't see? I unloosed my necktie, took a couple of deep breaths, and was able to regain my composure a little bit. I pressed myself against the wall and just stood there and listened. It was the strangest thing that I ever experienced in my life! I wondered if maybe I had stepped through some time warp and could really be in danger!

"I could hear some muffled conversation. It sounded like male voices barking out orders. Then a banging sound would accompany the heavy footsteps. None of it sounded natural at all. Whoever it was kept coming my way and I had no place to run. I was so scared that I could hardly breathe. I remained against the wall, hoping not to be noticed in case it passed me by. I was paralyzed with fear as the things moved closer and closer to where I was standing. This ghostly parade had to pass me and they had to see me standing there.

"Then, thank goodness, the sounds began to silence themselves until I heard nothing at all. Silence had never been so welcome! Slowly, my breathing began to return to normal. My eyes shifted from left to right and I stepped away from the wall that I'd braced myself against. I saw nothing in the dim light so I decided that it was safe to move to the center of the hallway and walk back.

"As I made my way back to my office, I was expecting to see something, though I don't know what. I just thought that there might be some trace of whatever had just been there. I was relieved to find nothing. I hurried down the hall to my office, glancing cautiously over my shoulder, but nothing else happened.

"When I reached my desk, I did not attempt to finish my work. I wasted no time turning off my computer! I fled the building without looking back. I have no plans to work alone in my office late in the evening ever again. That weird walk was quite enough for me!"

But are there others who do not have a choice? Are there still spirits imprisoned in that historic old building just as they were years ago? If not, then where do the moans and groans and footsteps come from? Are the answers in the moldy old tunnels beneath the Louisville streets or in the dimly lit hallways of the remodeled correctional facility? Is there anyone out there brave enough to go and see?

16. A PARANORMAL PARTY

Old Shackleton's Music Store
621 South Fourth Street

Growing up in Louisville instilled in me a deep fascination with the downtown buildings. There were a variety of interesting designs but, because I especially liked music, I was drawn to the old Shackleton's Music Store. It seemed to me that this store had some special power to attract people.

During my time as a youngster wearing jeans and sneakers, I would go downtown and stand gazing in the windows of the old store. I remember seeing the big, black shiny grand pianos displayed in these particular windows. I would imagine how they would end up in fancy ballrooms or on stages, providing spellbinding music for dancing or entertainment. At that age, I was sure that store would thrive there forever.

Today, only a shell remains of the old Shackleton's Music Store in busy downtown Louisville. Once it was filled with life and the joy that only music can bring to the living. Now the music has died, along with many of the people who came there long ago.

If the stories that I have heard over the past few years are true, then some of these people still come back from time to time. Now, I am told, the silence is broken by ghostly voices and the laughter of shadow people, searching perhaps for the haunting strains of music that they heard so long ago. Perhaps all of the changes and renovations that have occurred are as strange to them as their shadowy forms are to the living that have encountered them.

Who is haunting the old Shackleton's Music Store and why? As a grown-up leader of the downtown ghost walks, I wanted to learn all I could about the old place from a present-day prospective. Was there a solution to the mystery? Its appearance gives us no clues.

Unique in architecture design for a downtown landscape, the store has two large display areas enclosed with glass on two sides for street side viewing of

pianos and what looks like giant brass bells on top of the showcase windows. Nothing else compares to it downtown.

From a distance across the street, the exterior resembles that of a house painted in an orange hue. Black trim details the woodwork downstairs and the three upstairs windows look out in perfect alignment. A chandelier on the porch hangs down, suspended from the ceiling.

Inside the front door, a striking spiral staircase sweeps down from the second floor. A person could almost imagine seeing people from another time period descend that spiral staircase and be greeted with applause below.

The building has lost much of its historical integrity. During renovations of the adjoining Palace Theater, a wall was knocked down and openings were created to allow patrons to enjoy a concession area. A bar for drinks and snacks allows the guests to go from one venue to the other during intermission.

The outside parts of the building did not satisfy my curiosity about the mystique of the old place so I contacted the folks at Axxis Lighting and Sound, whose company had access to the building and who could take me on a tour inside. As it turned out, I got a ghostly "inside" story, too.

My guide was a woman with a thin face and a ponytail hairstyle. She didn't look like one who would be spooked easily.

"My company has the contract to provide lighting for theatrical productions, and the Palace Theater is one of the venues," she explained. "There is something about this place that is haunting and mysterious."

It was late afternoon when we visited the building but it wasn't totally dark inside. She pulled the keys from her pockets and we stepped just across the threshold. The setting sun created shadows of the window frames that appeared on the bare walls and near the spiral staircase. There was not a sound in the building as I waited for her to secure the door behind us.

We took a few steps, stopped, and looked around the building.

"I get an eerie feeling in here," I told her.

"I know what you mean," she replied, unzipping her jacket and taking a deep breath. "Would you like to hear what happened to one of my associates and me when we were in here not long ago?"

"Absolutely!" I said.

"I had the key to the front door that day," she said. "It has two locks, one at the top and one dead bolt just below the knob. I bolted the door and we were locked inside."

Her voice made me shiver and I listened intently as she continued.

"The building was dimly lit but we could see fairly well with the few security lights that were glowing. We didn't go far at all for in the far reaches of the building we saw them."

She hesitated and I urged her to go on.

"Saw what?" I asked, almost dreading her answer.

"At first," she said, "it looked like gray shadows, which surprised us. As our eyes adjusted, more and more shadows began to emerge -- one, two, three -- until it was almost a crowd. We not only heard the sounds of laughter and talking, but we could also hear the sounds of glasses tinkling together as if they were raising the glasses to toast one another."

"That's amazing!" I exclaimed.

She nodded in agreement and we began walking the length of the building, past the spiral staircase and the potted plants, beyond the bar that is parallel with an exterior wall, and past the few tables scattered about with their chairs turned upright. When we reached the area where she saw the shadow people, I stopped and allowed my eyes to explore my surroundings. She paced back and forth as she continued to recount her adventure to me.

"I couldn't believe my eyes," she said. "My associate and I turned and looked at each other, then back at those shadows, and finally back at each other. It looked like a cluster of shadows, or ghosts, were gathered here for some celebration. We didn't even walk as far as the spiral staircase before I began to feel coldness all around my feet."

"Where was it coming from?" I asked. "Do you think that it was from the party of ghosts?"

"I think so," she answered. "We started walking toward them and the coldness I felt started moving up toward my knees."

"How frightening!" I commented.

"It really did scare me," she said, "and I am not one to scare easily."

"Did they disappear then?" I asked.

"No," she answered. "As we moved closer, their voices and laughter intensified and it sounded as if it was coming closer and closer to us! I must have been traveling with the coldness, for it was creeping up past my knees and on to my hips. Neither of us said a word. It wasn't necessary! We knew that it was time to leave, and fast! We both turned around and scrambled to the door.

"We pushed on the door with all our might but it wouldn't budge. We were locked inside! My associate's hands were pressed flat against the panes of glass on the door and his face was just inches away.

"I fumbled for the keys but they flew from my hand and landed on the floor. I stooped down and started patting the black tile for the keys. I found that they had landed between my feet. As I picked them up, I realized that I was now completely engulfed by the cold. The ghostly conversations were loud and I could hear their mumbled voices. The metal keys that I was grasping now turned icy cold, too.

"Standing up, I finally managed to unlock both locks. As the door swung wide open, we stumbled and fell out onto the pavement. We lay sprawled out on the brick walkway, just shuddering."

I was shuddering, too, at this point.

"What happened then?" I ventured to ask.

"We just looked at each other as we raised up, without even stopping to brush ourselves off," she said. "He slammed the door closed and leaned against it with his feet firmly planted on the bricks. His eyes were wide open and he was breathing hard as I secured the two locks."

"How frightening!" I said.

"'What happened in there?' he asked me.

"'I don't know,' was all I could say.

"We both turned to the door and pressed our faces against the glass panes one last time. Whatever was going on in the back of the room was no longer visible. Maybe they were called back to another time period or dimension. I don't know."

"How long was it before you returned to this building?" I had to ask her.

"Oh, I wasn't in any hurry to return," she laughed. "I've been in here many times since, but I've never seen anything ghostly again."

As much as I wanted to solve the mystery of who was haunting the old store, I had to admit to myself that I was relieved that no ghosts had materialized to enlighten me during our tour.

But strange stories are repeated over and over like the chorus of a haunting melody. And inside of the Old Shackleton's Music Store, something or someone lurks and listens.

17. GHOSTS OF THE SEELBACH HOTEL

The Seelbach Hotel
500 South Fourth Street

If you were to check into the Seelbach Hotel today, you'd probably need a reservation. However, some guests come and go as they choose without any reservations at all. They stay as long as they want to and never even pay a cent. These guests are permanent residents and get special treatment because they are ghosts.

It is no wonder that anyone entering this magnificent old hotel would not be inclined to check out right away. The charm of its past and the high quality of its modern services draw people from all over the world.

Gangster Al Capone was a frequent guest of the hotel and brought along plenty of illegal liquor. Author F. Scott Fitzgerald stayed at the Seelbach and later used the hotel in a scene in his 1925 novel The Great Gatsby. Presidents Taft, Wilson, Franklin Roosevelt, Truman, Kennedy, Johnson, Carter, Clinton, and George W. Bush have all been guests. Other famous guests include Elvis Presley, Mikhail Gorbachev, Arnold Palmer, Jimmy Hoffa, Janet Jackson, Wolfgang Puck, Sarah Ferguson, Miss Piggy, and many, many more.

In 1905, this impressive Louisville landmark was built at the corner of 4th and Walnut Street (Muhammad Ali Blvd). It was just in time for the Seelbach to open its doors to receive guests for the 29th running of the Kentucky Derby. As business boomed for the hotel, its owners soon realized that an expansion project was needed. 1907 marked the finish of the southern side of the Seelbach Hotel. The hotel continued to flourish.

Then the hotel saw many changes over the years. Things became different in the city center and business declined. Eventually, the doors of the once grand Seelbach Hotel were closed, seemingly forever. During the 1970s, the property was abandoned. Plywood covered the doors and broken windows. But,

Outside of the Seelbach Hotel in 1885

eventually, the hotel gained supporters and was reopened in the early 1980s.

A few years after 1907, the Blue Lady made her first appearance at the Seelbach. You might say that she checked out in order to check in permanently!

It was her wedding day and a grand reception was held on the second floor, where the Oak Room is today. An array of flowers adorned the large arched windows, candles glowed on the tables, and a small brass ensemble waited to play for the bride and groom on their special day.

In the hallway of the 10th floor, the bride walked to the bridal suite to change for her reception. Only one thing was on her mind as she was headed to the suite, and that was how beautiful she'd look wearing her blue gown that had been specially made for her. She visualized stepping off of the elevator wearing that beautiful gown with her new husband by her side and how glorious they'd look arm in arm. Her thoughts drifted to the first dance as a married couple and receiving her family and friends at the reception.

But that wasn't to happen.

Opening the doors to her bridal suite where her husband was supposed to be waiting, she soon realized that he wasn't there. Puzzled, she called his name but she heard no response. Concerned, she went back to the hallway and began knocking on each door. She rattled the doorknobs and called his name but she got no answer.

Then she came upon one room with an unlocked door. With a light tap and a twist of the doorknob, she walked into the room to see if she could obtain some information about her husband's whereabouts. Unfortunately, she did but it was not what she wanted to know.

Apparently, the new husband was not quite ready to settle down with just

his new bride. He was not dressed in his wedding attire as his new bride had envisioned. He was in the arms of another woman. Their eyes met but no one spoke. The embrace said it all.

The young bride turned and ran from the room, slamming the door behind her. She rushed to the elevator and stood waiting for the door to open. Tears streamed down her face and she brushed them away with one arm across her forehead. Her hands clenched into fists, she banged on the elevator door. Where was it? Why was it taking so long?

Wanting to get away and not thinking clearly, she frantically forced open the elevator door. She stood looking down the 10 stories of long gray cables into the darkness below. Then she swayed and dropped to her death. But her story doesn't end here as her life ended.

Guests who have rooms on the 10th floor sometimes place calls to the front desk, alarmed about what they have heard and seen. They are experiences that they can't explain.

"When I turn out my light and get ready for bed, I keep hearing someone rattle the door," said one such guest. "I call out to see who is there but nobody answers."

One man reported, "I heard a woman's voice calling in the hallway. I opened my door and looked out but nobody was there."

"I opened my door thinking that someone was in distress but, looking up and down the hallway, I found nobody there," elaborated another guest.

Still another guest recounted a different story.

"As I was stepping off of the elevator, I looked down the hallway and saw a pale looking apparition of a woman, and she was coming my way! She had on a blue gown and she appeared to be floating on air. Her feet were not touching the carpet!"

Is this poor soul who has a heavy heart still roaming the 10th floor in the hopes of recapturing what was once lost? Nobody knows for she makes contact with nobody. Her thoughts are her own, suspended in time indefinitely.

Another lady ghost has left her imprint on the building in an unusual way. She is not an elegant lady in blue, but a bag lady in soiled, ill-fitting clothes. Nobody knows her connection to the hotel, but she seems to be attracted to one part especially.

Just inside of the lobby of the hotel to the left is Otto's Restaurant. Many businesses over the years, from restaurants to drugstores have occupied that prime location. Today, Otto's occupies that area and the name Otto's comes from Otto Seelbach, one of the previous owners.

When the hotel reopened in the early 1980s, a Southern Baptist Ministerial student worked there. He worked the graveyard shift and his main responsibility was getting the restaurant ready for the breakfast crowd. His tasks included wiping down the tables, brushing off the chairs, filling the salt and pepper shakers, sweeping the carpet, and cleaning the mirrors.

At that time, part of the décor included mirrors on three sides of the four walls. This made the otherwise small restaurant give the illusion of being larger than it actually was.

One night in January, this man was doing his job to the best of his ability. The hour was late and the hotel, being the dead of winter, was practically deserted. As he moved about cleaning the restaurant, he glanced up and looked into the mirror. Opposite of where he was standing with his back to the main entrance, he saw in the reflection of a bag lady. He stopped and just stared in the mirror, for he had not heard the door open. Now where did she come from and how did she get in? he thought. Didn't she realize that the restaurant isn't open for business at this hour?

He paid careful attention to her appearance down to the last detail. She was an old woman with gray hair, wearing an ill-fitting topcoat. Her shoes were large and worn and needed replacing. She carried her few treasures in a plain shopping bag, which she clutched with one hand. The clothes on her body were soiled. Her eyes were downcast toward the floor and she never looked his way. On her head was a crocheted hat, pulled down low on her ears.

As he watched her in the mirror, he slowly wiped down a table.

I'll just let her stay for a while to get warm, he thought. It's so cold outside! Besides, nobody will know. I'll just keep an eye on her in the mirrors.

This decided, he moved about the restaurant completing all of his tasks but, all the while, watching her in the mirrors. He looked away for just an instant to check his work and glanced up again, expecting to see her sitting by the door. To his amazement, she wasn't there!

He dropped the broom with a crack on the tiled floor as he whipped around to see where she had gone, but she had simply disappeared.

He raced out into the lobby of the building exclaiming, "Where did she go?"

The lobby was deserted! He stood in the center looking up toward the mezzanine but no one was in sight. He rushed over and leaned over the golden stair railing, looking down. Nobody was there.

"People just don't disappear," he mumbled to himself but, evidently, the bag lady had done just that.

He summoned the hotel security and, within seconds, the men from security found him standing in the center of the lobby with his hands in his pockets, looking puzzled.

"She was right here, sitting by the door," he explained to the guards. "I watched her in the mirrors as I moved about the restaurant. Then she was gone! Vanished! I don't know how to explain it because I never heard the door open or close."

The security guards wrote down all of the information given to them by the bewildered worker. They searched the hotel from the 10th floor down to the ground level to the Rathskellar, leaving no area unchecked. They came up empty-handed. There was no bag lady and no trace of her presence. There was no evidence at all.

"Whoever she was, she's gone now," stated one of the security guards. "She probably just slipped in to get warm and then slipped out again."

The security officers filed the report and the young man went back and completed his work for the night. Time passed and they all forgot about the old bag lady. The young ministerial student moved on.

Another January arrived and another Southern Baptist ministerial student was hired to work in the restaurant. Like the first young student, this one had the job of preparing the restaurant for the breakfast crowd. He had no knowledge of what had happened the year before.

The hour was late on this very cold January night. The young worker was grateful to be inside on such a night as he moved about wiping down the chairs and tables. He paused for a moment, just long enough to tuck his shirt into his pants. Then, he glanced into the mirror to check his appearance and stopped dead still. He couldn't believe what he saw.

"A bag lady!" he said to himself. "Now where did she come from?"

He was unsure about what to do, but he couldn't see any harm in allowing her to sit inside long enough to get warm. He decided to go over and speak to her.

As he turned and began walking in her direction, she vanished right in front of his eyes. He stood blinking for a few seconds to make sure that he was seeing right. The he raced to the lobby.

"People don't just disappear!" he said to himself. "She has to be around here somewhere."

Moving quickly into the lobby, he looked behind each marble column. Then he stood at the bottom of the grand staircase and looked toward the mezzanine level. The old bag lady was nowhere to be seen.

"I'm too busy for games," he mumbled. "If she's hiding, security can find her and throw her out."

The only sound heard was his own footsteps as he walked across the marble floor to reach the concierge's telephone.

Security responded to his call within seconds and he explained about seeing the mysterious old bag lady in the restaurant. They listened as he elaborated on her unkempt appearance and the shopping bag that she was carrying.

"Wait a minute," said one of the security guards. "We had something just like this last year."

He returned to the office and came back with the manila folder containing the notes from last year's investigation.

"Look," said the guard. "It says that the woman had gray hair and was wearing a crocheted hat like you just described."

They soon realized that the woman the young worker had just described was the same woman who was seen last year. The guard pointed out that, according to their notes, the time of the appearance of the bag lady this year was the same as the year before and that it was exactly one year later to the date.

Hotel security again searched the building from top to bottom, end to end. Their search was fruitless, for no trace of this woman was found.

In the course of the hotel's operations, the decision was made to remove the mirrors in the restaurant. Next on the plan was to enlarge the restaurant and completely redecorate with a new color scheme and wall accent pieces. When the mirrors came down, people talked and felt like they would never see the bag lady again. They were wrong! She hasn't left the Seelbach at all.

Guests and employees alike have reported fleeting encounters with her. Some may be waiting for an elevator and others may be in the restroom checking their appearance when they pause to glance in the mirror. Expecting to see their own reflection, they become startled to see something quite different. Standing in the background will be the reflection of a bag lady. They turn to confront her only to find nobody there. Then they'll look back in the mirror and she will be standing there again. There is never a sound. No footsteps are heard to signal the entrance or exit of another person.

Is she someone who could once afford to stay in the grand hotel? Is she a vagrant who might have gained access to the hotel during the time that it was boarded up and abandoned? Or is she just a lost, lonely spirit who is drawn by the warmth? For now, we have no answers.

If you ever decide to visit the Seelbach, perhaps their two lady ghosts will be there to greet you. Unlike other guests of the hotel who come and go, The Blue Lady and The Bag Lady never check out.

ABOUT THE AUTHOR

Robert Parker, a native of Louisville, Kentucky, makes his home in south Louisville, just in the shadows of the twin spires of Churchill Downs. By profession, he is a middle school teacher in Jefferson County with expertise in the field of computer technology and reading. Among the students at school, he is known as the "teacher with all the lighthouse pictures and who tells ghost stories".

With a growing interest in the paranormal, he has always had a fascination with ghost stories that are historical and can be traced back to real people. "Historical storytelling is a great educational tool that does spark interest in local history" is one of his professional beliefs.

Having visited over 200 lighthouses along the Atlantic and the Great Lakes, he has met countless individuals who have experienced paranormal activity and heard their stories surrounding the legends and the sea. Other interests include theater, traveling, performing with the Thoroughbred Chorus, and just about any activity outdoors where people meet and mingle.

If you've had an encounter with some ghosts in a downtown Louisville property, feel free to contact the writer. Offering new stories is what keeps the ghost walking tours alive and well, and the reassurance that you aren't alone makes all the difference in the world.

Robert W. Parker
502-367-1664
LouGhstWalks@aol.com

LOUISVILLE GHOST WALKS

From May until October, author Robert Parker hosts the popular Ghost Walks of Downtown Louisville! The tour departs each Friday night from the first floor lobby of the Brown Hotel at the corner of 4th and Broadway, in downtown Louisville. Stories and stops on the tour include haunted sites from this book:

- The Brown Hotel: Will you come face to face with Mr. Brown himself? He has been seen all throughout the building, from the kitchen to the upper floors.
- The Brennan House: Here, tour goers have claimed to see the apparition of a man peering down at them from the upstairs windows. Will you be one of those who have seen this ghost?
- The Palace Theater: Just how many spirits haunt this grand old movie theater? Some tour attendees have been touched, pushed and had their hair pulled at this haunted site.
- The Seelbach Hotel: Rub shoulders with the ghosts of the Seelbachs former guests, from F. Scott Fitzgerald to Al Capone. How many may be lingering still?

- And many other sites are included on your spirited journey! The cost of the tour is $10 for adults and $5 for children. Reservations are required for all tours. Special private tours may also be arranged by reservation. Dont wait because the tours fill up fast! Call Mr. Ghost Walker today at (502) 689-5117 or visit us online at

http://www.louisvilleghostwalks.com

WHITECHAPEL PRESS

Whitechapel Productions Press is a division of Dark Haven Entertainment and a small press publisher, specializing in books about ghosts and hauntings. Since 1993, the company has been one of America's leading publishers of supernatural books and has produced such best-selling titles as Haunted Illinois, The Ghost Hunters Guidebook, Ghosts on Film, Confessions of a Ghost Hunter, Resurrection Mary, Bloody Chicago, The Haunting of America, Spirits of the Civil War and many others.

With nearly a dozen different authors producing high quality books on all aspects of ghosts, hauntings and the paranormal, Whitechapel Press has made its mark with America's ghost enthusiasts.

Whitechapel Press is also the publisher of the acclaimed **Ghosts of the Prairie** magazine, which started in 1997 as one of the only ghost-related magazines on the market. It continues today as a travel guide to the weird, haunted and unusual in Illinois. Each issue also includes a print version of the Whitechapel Press ghost book catalog.

You can visit Whitechapel Productions Press online and browse through our selection of ghostly titles, plus get information on ghosts and hauntings, haunted history, spirit photographs, information on ghost hunting and much more. by visiting the internet website at:

www.prairieghosts.com

Or call us toll-free at 1-888-446-7859 to order any of our titles.
Discounts are available to retail outlets and online booksellers!

ILLINOIS AND AMERICAN HAUNTINGS TOURS

Whitechapel Press (and Dark Haven Entertainment) is the headquarters for the Illinois Hauntings Tour Co, offering the following ghost tours:

Weird Chicago Tours / Chicago, Illinois
Created by Troy Taylor and based on his book Weird Illinois from Barnes & Noble Press, this is an alternative tour of Chicago, offering visitors the chance to see the other side of the city. Visit Chicagos most haunted sites, most notorious crime spots, most unusual places and much more! Available all year round!
http://www.weirdchicago.com

Haunted Decatur Ghost Tours / Decatur, Illinois
Created by Troy Taylor in 1994, these are the third longest running ghost tours in the state of Illinois! Visit the citys most haunted spots and take a nightime stroll through Greenwood Cemetery! Available April - October!
http://www.haunteddecatur.com

Alton Hauntings Ghost Tours / Alton, Illinois
Created by Troy Taylor, these tours are an interactive experience that allow readers to visit the historically haunted locations of the city and can be booked every year from April through October. Hosted by Len Adams, Luke Naliborski & Troy Taylor ---
http://www.altonhauntings.com

American Hauntings Ghost Tours
Created by author Troy Taylor these tours offer Haunted Overnight Excursions to ghostly places around the Midwest and throughout the country. Available all year round!
http://www.illinoishauntings.com

Springfield Hauntings Ghost Tours / Springfield, Illinois
Join us in the Prairie States haunted Capital City for Springfields only authentic ghost tours. Experience the hauntings of Abraham Lincoln, the Springfield Theater Center and much more! Available April through October and hosted by John Winterbauer ----
http://www.springfieldhauntings.com

CPSIA information can be obtained at www.ICGtesting.com
Printed in the USA
LVOW10s0609070916

503482LV00014B/80/P